A CASEBOOK ON
HAROLD PINTER'S
The Homecoming

A CASEBOOK ON
HAROLD PINTER'S
The Homecoming

Edited by
John Lahr and Anthea Lahr

DAVIS-POYNTER
LONDON

First published in Great Britain in 1974 by
Davis-Poynter Ltd, 20 Garrick Street,
London WC2E 9BJ

ISBN 0 7067 0128 3

An earlier version of 'A Woman's Place' by Bernard F.
Dukore was first published in *Quarterly Review of Speech,*
LII, October 1966; an earlier version of 'Pinter the Space-
man' by John Lahr was first published in *Evergreen Review*
No. 55, June 1968; both are printed by permission.

Printed in Great Britain by
Compton Printing Ltd Aylesbury Bucks

To Harold Pinter: in admiration
and
For Anthea: "One of the few and far between"

Acknowledgments

This book could not have been created without the help of many people who share a deep enthusiasm and appreciation for Harold Pinter and his work. I am grateful for the conversations, advice, and the helping hands offered me by Henry Woolf, John Kershaw, Martin Esslin, Terence Rigby, Paul Rogers, John Bury, Fred Jordan, and especially Irving Wardle who so generously donated much time and energy to being a trans-atlantic liaison.

To my wife, Anthea, I owe a special cheese roll. She not only chased down permissions and typed the manuscript, but edited the hours of taped interviews.

All quotations from *The Homecoming* are from the edition published by Grove Press, Inc., 1966.

Contents

THE HOMECOMING was first presented by the Royal Shakespeare Company at the Aldwych Theatre on June 3, 1965, with the following cast:

MAX, *a man of seventy*	Paul Rogers
LENNY, *a man in his early thirties*	Ian Holm
SAM, *a man of sixty-three*	John Normington
JOEY, *a man in his middle twenties*	Terence Rigby
TEDDY, *a man in his middle thirties*	Michael Bryant
RUTH, *a woman in her early thirties*	Vivien Merchant

Directed by Peter Hall

The first American production opened at The Music Box on January 5, 1967. With the exception of the part of Teddy, which was played by Michael Craig, the cast was as above.

INTRODUCTION

John Lahr

Man cannot live without a sense of the secret. . . .
But the invasion of technique desacrilizes the world
in which man is called upon to live. For technique
nothing is sacred, there is no mystery, no taboo. . . .
      —Jacques Ellul, *The Technological Society*

Harold Pinter is the finest playwright to emerge in our technological society; and it is ironic that the humanity of his vision is achieved by bringing audiences back to an awareness of the inherent mystery of people and objects. This is his obsession; and he pursues it with ruthless dedication. The act of writing is as much a process of discovery for him as following the protean moods and motives of his characters is for the audience.

> My characters tell me so much and no more, with reference to their experience, their aspirations, their motives, their history. Between my lack of biographical data about them and the ambiguity of what they say there lies a territory which is not only worthy of exploration but which it is compulsory to explore. You and I, the characters which grow on a page, most of the time we're inexpressive, giving little away, unreliable, elusive, evasive, obstructive, unwilling. But it's out of these attributes that a language arises. . . .*

---

* *Sunday Times* (London). March 4, 1962. Pinter's speech to the Seventh National Student Drama Festival in Bristol.

xi

While Pinter dramatizes the ambiguity of language and man's penchant for evasion, his plays are never vague or murky. The realism of his work has the weight of such meticulous observation and control that this precision elevates it to the abstract. The audience is conscious of entering a world in which every prop and plot point exists in an electric, precarious balance. Pinter is creating a world as mercurial as the imagination itself. His moral "statement" is not in the mouths of his characters, but in his refusal to "cheat" * an audience by limiting the theatrical experience to false simplicity or easy sentiment:

> If I write about a lamp I apply myself to the demands of that lamp. If I write about a flower, I apply myself to the demands of that flower. In most cases, the flower has singular properties as opposed to the lamp. . . . Flower, lamp, tin-opener, tree . . . tend to take alteration from different climate and circumstance and I must necessarily attend to that singular change with the same devotion and allowance. . . .
>
> I am not trying to assert myself when I write, or rarely. [My subjects] present themselves to me in their separate guises. I sharpen my tools for them. I stand them in front of the window with the light behind them, I place them in a corner in the shadows. I am there, of course—I am writing the stuff. There are many corridors and many rooms, many climates, in my possession. I am not a fixed star. Of course I am there—everywhere—I crawl on all fours—I declare war—I abdicate—it is my world. But I do not sit in a cosy didactic corner in *one* room, speaking through a loudspeaker. My preoccupation is not a cosy corner. It is the house.**

---

* Pinter: "The explicit form which is so often taken in twentieth-century drama is . . . cheating. The playwright assumes that we have a great deal of information about all his characters, who explain themselves to the audience. In fact, what they are doing most of the time is conforming to the author's own ideology." As quoted in Martin Esslin, *The Peopled Wound: The Works of Harold Pinter*, Methuen, London, 1970, p.38.

** *Ibid.*, pp. 227–228.

The Homecoming (1965) is Pinter's major full-length work,
a triumph of craftsmanship and artistic intention. Here, in
the cavernous main room of Max's house, Pinter compresses
the masks of language, the terror of identity, the instability
of our notion of the past which are his main concerns. Visually,
the room is cleaner, more spare than Aston's cluttered bed-
sitter in *The Caretaker* (1960), or the chintzy cosiness of
Meg's seaside boarding house in *The Birthday Party* (1958).
The language, also, has been honed down; its resonance
opened up with a much more daring, rigorous use of the
pause and the silence. *The Homecoming* is a brilliantly sculpted
stage event. The audience is forced to focus on the impact of
the *moment*. In such a minimal environment, every gesture
and word counts for something. The drama and terror Pinter
feels in the world need not be the bravura shock tactics of
Stanley's blindman's buff in *The Birthday Party* nor Mick's
overt role-playing in *The Caretaker*. In *The Homecoming*,
Pinter has refined his stage image. The fusion between word–
gesture–environment is startling; the tension becomes volcanic.
In this climate, simple actions have a tantalizing suggestiveness.
As Pinter has said:

> The world is full of surprises. A door can open at any
> moment and someone will come in. We'd love to know
> who it is, we'd love to know exactly what he has on his
> mind and why he comes in, but how often do we know
> what someone has on his mind or who this somebody is,
> and what goes to make him and make him what he is,
> and what his relationship is to others? *

In *The Homecoming*, this sense of surprise is heightened
by the space and silence which etch every moment. The
audience knows as much about the characters as the characters do about themselves. They too struggle to differentiate
between fact and fantasy, to *remember* a strand of information

---

* *Ibid.*, p. 38–39.

that may or may not be part of their history; yet, in so far as it is *believed to be true*, it *is true*.

Pinter works hard to achieve intimacy between audience and stage image. The appeal of Pinter's technique of playing is as simple as it is rivetting: a riddle the audience must solve. The silences and pauses focus the audience's attention on the words, giving language a new amperage and mystery. Words are shown in their actuality: instruments which both reveal and conceal. The audience must listen beneath the words for what is really being said; at the same time, action becomes as unpredictable as it is *irrevocable*. The shock of immediacy is part of Pinter's vision of theater.

> I'm not suggesting that no character in a play can ever say what he in fact means. Not at all. I have found that there invariably does come a moment when this happens, where he says something, perhaps, which he has never said before. And where this happens, what he says is irrevocable, and can never be taken back.*

The audience cannot anticipate any character's next move. This is not melodrama whose formula beginning, middle and end assures us of life's coherence; Pinter's stage illusion brings the audience dangerously close to the instinctive motive force behind *any* act. All the characters in *The Homecoming* are taken by the surprise of the moment. Lenny's immodest proposal to Ruth is countered by words which momentarily knock him off his pins:

LENNY: I'll take it, then.
RUTH: If you take the glass . . . I'll take you.
    Pause.
LENNY: How about me taking the glass without you taking me?
RUTH: Why don't I just take you?
    Pause.
LENNY: You're joking.
    Pause.

---

* *Sunday Times, op. cit.*

Even Max, in all his gruff bravado, is talking of a surrogate cook and bottlewasher until Lenny suggests another alternative. Max's mocking enthusiasm cannot hide his surprise.

LENNY: . . . . Why don't I take her up with me to Greek Street?
Pause.
MAX: You mean put her on the game?
Pause.
We'll put her on the game. . . . You mean she can earn the money herself—on her back?

Within the pauses, the audience witnesses the visceral process of decision: the characters are hiding, judging, rallying, redefining. Balanced on the crest of the irrational, each action sweeps down with an awesome impact. Things are said and done in life out of a network of motives too complicated to explain: only hints are possible, but the gestures themselves have a compelling size and irrevocable consequence. Sam's confession; Ruth's roll on the sofa with Joey; her decision to form a new community are vivid wounds to the imaginations of the characters. Memory will blur and transform these betrayals in the same way that Jessie's infamous history has been confused in Max's mind. Even the audience, inundated with data about the family, will take away only fragmentary images of the event. *The Homecoming* dramatizes this paradox of knowledge more powerfully than Pinter's other plays. Reality slips away like sand under foot; but the gullible mind clutches at any straw for the illusion of coherence.

I

Pinter has talked a great deal about *the room* and its symbolic significance. This prophesies our technological stand-off: man receding increasingly into the circumference not only of his room, but his mind.

. . . . I'm dealing with these characters at the extreme edge of their living, where they are living pretty much alone, at their hearth, their home hearth. . . .*

Outside the room is a modern world moving at stupefying speed; a technological society whose change forces the characters to seek the safety, familiarity, and consolation of their "home hearth." Science battles the unknown; but its victories are generally uncomprehended and no solace from the despair of the moment. Technology "frees" man from coping with other men. This loss of contact breeds the ignorance and isolation which feeds fear and violence. Nature, in Pinter's plays, is now only a memory: a name to be dropped with passing irony. The landscape outside the room is barren. *The Homecoming* is haunted by this profound sense of death. In this climate of freakish instability, it is no accident that Max (as Lenny says) is "obsessed with order and clarity." The confusion and pain outside the room are brought inside through the characters' method of evading them. Pinter has said:

I mean, there comes a point, surely, where the living in *the* world must be tied up with living in *your own* world, where you are—in your room . . . Before you manage to adjust to living alone in your room . . . you are not terribly fit and equipped to go out and fight the battles . . . which are mostly in abstractions in the outside world.**

Max, the butcher, knows about slaughter; and his brutality to others has been nurtured in a world familiar with annihilation. Death becomes a *positive* value. Max is numb to the spectacle of destruction.

MAX: He didn't even fight in the war. This man didn't even fight in the bloody war!

---

* Esslin, *op. cit.,* p. 34.
** *Ibid,* p. 34.

SAM: I did!
MAX: Who did you kill?
   Silence.

Mockery is the only tone which straight-arms the sense of destruction and loss. The abrasion outside and inside the room has eroded the characters' humanity and made them insensate. For instance, Sam keels over. There seems to be a sudden death in the family.

MAX: What's he done? Dropped dead?
LENNY: Yes.
MAX: A corpse? A corpse on my floor? Get him out of here! Clear him out of here!
   JOEY *bends over* SAM.
JOEY: He's not dead.
LENNY: He probably was dead, for about thirty seconds.
MAX: He's not even dead!

In the tone—the outrageousness of it—is a psychic withdrawal, a spiritual closing-off. This spiritual stalemate is prophetic of the emotional shifts in western society since World War II. Viewing his diminished destiny, man may laugh bitterly or seek revenge; but there is, at its base, a sense of a moral vacuum as blatant as Ruth's violent, casual dismissal of her husband.

RUTH: Eddie.
   TEDDY *turns*.
   Pause.
   Don't become a stranger.

The sense of loss, the inner rage at what has been left to the living, creates the powerful defense mechanisms of indifference and irony Pinter incarnates on stage. Psychiatrists have diagnosed this reaction to a world where there is no solace from daily catastrophe. Robert Jay Lifton has written about the *psychic numbing* which this play epitomizes.

It is protection against overwhelming and unacceptable stimuli, and it is associated with an inner imagery that goes something like this: "If I feel nothing, then death is not taking place"; or, "If I feel nothing, I cannot be threatened by death all around me"; or, "If I feel nothing, then I am not responsible for you and your death."*

The Homecoming offers no solutions, only a process. The continual change Pinter creates on stage mirrors the condition of instability off it. No value—not even family—is fixed and final. *The Homecoming* dramatizes the loss of Man's sense of his roots. The characters reach out for a past they cannot find. They are adrift; and violence is an indication of their confusion and loneliness. Life holds no continuity. Human consciousness, as *The Homecoming* so brilliantly demonstrates, is "a great emptiness, a wind blowing toward objects."**

II

The gorgeousness of *The Homecoming* rests with its elusive, hard truth. Pinter is wrestling with his own sense of spiritual dislocation and finding mirrors for ours. No biography can plumb *The Homecoming*'s essential mystery; no criticism can encompass all its nuances. Pinter, like the world his characters inhabit, is himself in a constant state of change. His latest one-act plays, *Landscape* and *Silence* (1968–1969), are an attempt to move his drama even further into the minds of his characters. "I felt that after *The Homecoming* . . . I couldn't any longer stay in the room with this bunch of people who opened doors and came in and went out. . . ."†

In its scope and variety, *The Homecoming* remains Pinter's most forceful and far-reaching vision. What follows is a

---

* Robert Jay Lifton, *Boundaries*, Random House, New York, 1970, p. 32.
** Jean-Paul Sartre as quoted in *ibid.*, p. 49.
† Esslin, *op. cit.*, p. 20.

casebook of a play already acknowledged as one of the major contributions to the theater of this century. The book is divided between the practical and the theoretical, a discussion and not a summing up. As a man of the theater, Pinter's choices come from an actor's sense of the people he writes about, as well as a practical sense of the stage. Criticism rarely has an opportunity to be read along with the concrete details of a production. One does not cancel out the other, but only stresses their unique and symbiotic relationship. Criticism, at its best, embodies the articulate audience, the fourth part in the equation of theater. It is especially pertinent to *The Homecoming* which stands at the zenith of contemporary stagecraft. "That's not equivocal, it's unequivocal."

THE HOMECOMING: AN INTERPRETATION

Martin Esslin

The Homecoming—Pinter's third full-length work, far more complex, richly textured and challenging than its predecessors —brought the playwright the most brilliant success of his career so far, winning praise not only in London's West End, but on Broadway as well.

The external action of the play seems simple enough: Max, a seventy-year-old retired butcher, lives in a large old house in a North London working-class district with his two sons, Lenny and Joey. Joey, the younger, works for a wrecking company and is an enthusiastic amateur boxer. He is rather slow witted and naïve. Lenny, on the other hand, is suave and intelligent; his profession remains, throughout the early scenes of the play, obscure. Max's brother Sam, a chauffeur for a car-rental agency, is the fourth inhabitant of the house. Max talks a good deal about his late wife Jessie, as well as of a friend of his, dead for some years, named MacGregor. Max, whose sons are extremely rude to him, is in charge of the household—above all, the kitchen. He has to put up with frequent complaints about the quality of the food.

Late one night, when these four have gone to bed, unannounced guests arrive. A third son, Teddy—the eldest son who, for the past six years, has been teaching philosophy at an American university—brings his wife Ruth into the family home. He hasn't yet introduced Ruth to his family; they are on their way back to America after vacationing in Italy. Since Teddy still has his house key, the unexpected visitors enter without being

noticed, at first, by anyone. A surprise meeting between Lenny
and Ruth then occurs, in the course of which Lenny talks in a
show-off manner about himself, without disclosing his profession, using language which, moreover, mysteriously combines
cultivated, even rather high-flown, English with the coarsest
slang. Two of Lenny's longer tales concern brutal acts com-
mitted against women—one a whore Lenny beat up because
she had tried to proposition him and he was sure she was diseased; the other, an old woman who once asked him to move
a heavy iron mangle from one room to another for her and then
didn't help him. Ruth's reaction is surprising in that she not
only accepts these weird tales as completely natural but also
starts provoking Lenny erotically.

The next morning when Max is introduced to his daughter-
in-law, he assumes she's a whore and furiously demands she get
out of the house at once. "I've never had a whore under this
roof before. Ever since your mother died. My word of honour."
Only after hearing that Ruth is a mother and has three small
sons in America does Max permit her to stay.

After lunch, the whole family is assembled. Max tells about
his married life with Jessie in great detail, Teddy about his work
as a philosophy professor. Lenny challenges Teddy to a discussion of philosophical questions, into which, however, Teddy
refuses to get drawn. Ruth then enters the conversation, turning
a question about the essence of a table into a question of what
is reality—her legs and her lips, for example. It is obvious that
she is offering herself to Lenny.

Teddy has decided to return to America somewhat earlier
than planned. Ruth seems to want to stay on. When Teddy
goes up to pack, Ruth's seduction of Lenny becomes increasingly
overt. She mentions that, before Teddy married her (just
before leaving for America), she had been a photographer's
model—a model, she intimates, for nude photos. When her
husband comes back downstairs, Ruth is kissing Lenny. When
the other brother, Joey, comes in and sees this, he shouts to his
father: "Christ, she's wide open. Dad, look at that. She's a

tart." After which, Joey embraces Ruth and gets her down on the sofa.

Two hours later: Ruth and Joey have gone upstairs together. Teddy is ready to leave. When Joey comes downstairs again, Lenny, in Teddy's presence, asks Joey how he made out with Ruth. Joey complains that she's "a tease." Teddy listens to the whole discussion with complete equanimity and even contributes a few remarks. When Max enters, his first question is, "Where's the whore? Still in bed? She'll make us all animals."

Max later suggests that Ruth should stay on in London with the family. Though Teddy protests that she's married and has three children, his protest is perfunctory. Lenny—who, as it turns out, lives off a stable of whores—takes up and expands on Max's suggestion: Ruth could contribute to the household expenses by working as a whore in Soho. Lenny asks Teddy, who follows the whole discussion in silence, if he could help out by recommending Ruth's services to London-bound American professors. Teddy's only reaction is, "She'd get old . . . very quickly."

But when Ruth comes downstairs, it is Teddy who tells her the family's proposal. Ruth listens to the proposal that she should contribute to the family budget by setting herself up as a whore as if it were the most natural thing in the world. She does make some tough financial conditions, however: a three-room flat, a maid, and her wardrobe to be paid for by Lenny. When Lenny agrees to her conditions, Ruth accepts the arrangement.

Sam, the uncle of the three brothers, who has been following the conversation with mounting excitement, suddenly gets up and cries out, "MacGregor had Jessie in the back of my cab as I drove them along," and collapses. Though he seems to have had a heart attack, the others pay little attention to him and leave him lying where he fell. In a very off-hand, casual manner, Teddy says goodbye to Ruth, and leaves.

Ruth remains. She strokes Joey's hair. Lenny stands by, not saying a word. Sam lies as if dead on the floor. And now Max, the old father, begs Ruth, in his turn, for her sexual favors. He's not as old as she thinks, he says. He falls to his knees and whimpers, "I'm not an old man. . . . Do you hear me? . . . Kiss me." Ruth goes on stroking Joey's hair. Lenny looks on, saying nothing. The curtain falls.

The Homecoming is a profoundly shocking play not only because it shows the transformation of an apparently completely respectable woman into a whore, but also, and chiefly, because the person most affected by this change accepts it with such complete nonchalance. One commonly heard criticism of the play is that, in reality, people to whom such things happen would react more violently, that Pinter's play is simply not credible.

A play like *The Homecoming*, however, the action of which takes place mainly on a surreal plane—the plane on which Kafka's *The Trial* or Beckett's *Waiting for Godot* happen—is by no means obliged to comply with all the rules of a naturalistic verisimilitude. Nonetheless, even on the level of a real event taking place in North London, it is completely credible. One must simply keep in mind Pinter's refusal to define his characters fully in the exposition or to present his audience with a detailed history of events leading up to the action as, for instance, Ibsen would. If one keeps in mind that Pinter's characters do not necessarily tell us the truth, but often no more than fantasies, lies, and self-deceptions about their previous history, one may then reconstruct the plot of the play on the plane of external reality as follows:

Above all, in the light of Sam's final outburst, Jessie—the mother of the three young men, Max's wife, whom Max depicts as part madonna—like Mother figure, part slut—may be seen as having been an adultress at the very least, but probably also a whore. Max's outburst on first meeting Ruth—that since the day Jessie died no whore has ever been in his house—is ambiguous but can also be understood to mean that Jessie herself was a whore. Teddy therefore, whose calm acceptance of the proposal that his wife should turn whore is so shocking to audiences, also grew up in a house in which both prostitution and talk about it were ordinary everyday events. Furthermore, he married Ruth in England before leaving for America and did not then introduce her to his father and brothers for the probable reason, that, after their mother's death, they would not have accepted her. Ruth was after all, as she herself states, a nude model, and thus not much better than a whore. Max, who must have an eye for such things, immediately recognizes Ruth as a potential prostitute when he meets her six years after her marriage to Teddy.

Moreover, Ruth is obviously a nymphomaniac. In his six years as her husband, Teddy must have become all too painfully *because* aware of this—thus his unruffled calm when he discovers her *Mk* in his brother's arms. If Ruth were a whore before he married her, and if there had been frequent evidence of her nymphomania during the six years of their marriage, if the trip to Venice was a last desperate attempt to save the marriage—an attempt that failed—then one can sympathize with Teddy's relief at not having to take Ruth back to America with him. In the narrow gossip-ridden milieu of a small American university (the milieu of Albee's *Who's Afraid of Virginia Woolf?*), she must have given him a good deal of trouble. Therefore he accepts her return to a whore's life as a relatively satisfactory solution. That Ruth is "sick" he mentions early on in the play. Thus the family in *The Homecoming* is an abnormal family, Ruth a nymphomaniac—but neither such people nor such developments as those that occur in the play are all that rare, not to say utterly impossible.

It is characteristic of Pinter's mature style that his plays are simultaneously real and surreal; it is precisely this double aspect of the events portrayed, their total ambivalence, which constitutes the strong poetic appeal of this type of drama, the impossibility, in short, of being able to verify where reality ends and the dream begins. ("Is my life being dreamed or is it true?" in the words of the old German lyric.) *The Homecom-*

ing is *also* a dream—the son's fantasy-dream of the sexual conquest of his mother.

Looking at the play's action from the point of view of the two younger sons, Lenny and Joey (who may be seen as two aspects of one personality), Max the father and Teddy the eldest brother are, in turn, different aspects of the same Father figure. Max is the father as a senile old man; Teddy, the father as the wiser, better-informed authority. The two brothers' antagonism toward Teddy is equally strong as their antagonism to Max. Further, if one regards Teddy as an aspect of the Father figure, his wife and sexual partner Ruth becomes a Mother figure. Ruth too, like Jessie, the mother of the three brothers, has three sons who, since Teddy and Ruth have only been married for six years, must be between two and five years old. One could also put it this way: For Lenny and Joey, Ruth is the image they had of their mother when they were children of two and five. In their sexual fantasies, the sons dream of their mother as a whore—in other words, as an easily available sexual object. Throughout literature we find a recurrent ambivalence of the image of Woman as both Mother, Madonna, and Whore. Thus, too, in Max's stories about Jessie, she sometimes emerges as a slut, at other times as a madonna-like Mother figure. The sons' fantasy dream (in Freud's classic description of the Oedipus complex) is of the conquest of the mother as a sexual object and of the simultaneous bringing down, by murder, of the father. The closing tableau of *The Homecoming* shows the father down on his knees begging for the favors of the Mother figure while both sons look on unmoved, and the Mother figure herself, unresponsive to his pleas, continues stroking the hair of one of her sons. Within the atmosphere of a fantasy dreamed by the sons, the unquestioning readiness with which Teddy and Ruth agree to the plan to prostitute Ruth appears completely natural. Only in dreams do things readily happen which one subconsciously always desired but knew to be unobtainable. Only in dreams do all obstacles give way at the slightest touch.

This interpretation of *The Homecoming* also yields some

insights into some of Pinter's other works. The closing scenes of *The Homecoming* and *The Caretaker* are, for example, strikingly similar. In the one case, an old man driven out of the house by two young men; in the other, an old man begging his two sons in vain for the sexual favors of a Mother figure. One sees that, in the last analysis, *The Caretaker* also deals with a father-son conflict: the sons give an old man a chance to adjust to a new situation, to being dominated by now fully-grown sons; he is defeated because he continues to think of himself as their superior, because he still imagines he possesses authority over them. Not only is there a clear parallel between Davies and Max (after all, Max acts as a kind of caretaker for Lenny and Joey; he cooks and keeps house; he is as talkative and deceitful as Davies), but Mick and Aston also closely correspond to Lenny and Joey. True, Mick's profession is never expressly stated, but he could easily be making his living off prostitutes. Lenny talks about fixing up apartments around London for his stable of whores; Mick's purchase of a run-down house, his plan to convert it into a luxury dwelling, could easily fit into the same general theme. Like Aston, Joey is, compared to Lenny, dull, a manual laborer and a boxer, an innocent simpleton.

In *The Birthday Party*, Stanley embodies the aspect of the dreamy artist unequipped to cope with the world. And Stanley is brutally torn away from a nearly incestuous relationship with a Mother figure. Thus one may regard Pinter's three full-length plays as a linked evolutionary series: in *The Birthday Party* the son is torn away from a Mother figure by a Father figure, Goldberg (whose mendacity and loquacity are strongly reminiscent of Davies and Max). In *The Caretaker*, the (divided) Son figure is powerful enough to expel the Father figure from the home. In *The Homecoming* the Mother figure is, for the first time, presented as a real sexual object and the downfall of the Father figure is more explicitly shown; in the third play the (divided) Son figure triumphs completely.

From this perspective some of Pinter's other works become, in many respects, more comprehensible. Albert in *A Night*

Out confronts a divided Mother-Whore figure; the mute match-seller in *A Slight Ache*, whom Flora takes to bed instead of her husband, could be a Son figure (well disguised·by the dream-censor) who dreams of taking his father's place in his mother's bed. In *Night School*, a son (Walter) fights with a Father figure (Solto) for possession of a girl who is a teacher by day but a night-club hostess at night—in other words, a whore. And in *The Lover*, the husband's need to see his wife also as a whore at times is vividly dramatized.

It must be emphasized, however, that such psychoanalytical explanations say nothing about Pinter's conscious intention or design as a playwright. As we know, Pinter's working method is completely intuitive; he sketches situations, delineates images which preoccupy, haunt, and obsess him. But it is just such over-intense daydreams as these which, springing from the author's subconscious mind, reveal subconscious material which demands psychoanalytic interpretation. On the spectator, these images which spring from the unconscious also exercise an effect which transcends the merely conscious sphere. An understanding of the underlying archetypes, which are here put before us on the stage, explains at least partially the strong effect such plays as *The Homecoming* have, even though, or precisely because, the audience leaves the theater bewildered, often even outraged, by what they have seen. Naturally, Pinter's plays contain much that is immediately fascinating, entertaining, and amusing: the brilliance of the dialogue, the precision of the nuances and overtones of language, the strong and surprising situations and *coups de théâtre*, the sharply drawn eccentric characters. Yet all these elements are fused by the poetic power of the basic situation itself, by the mysterious appeal of the archetypes which, in these complex patterns—existing on the levels of dream and of reality at one and the same time—touch those depths which are the innermost source of all poetry.

A DIRECTOR'S APPROACH

An Interview with Peter Hall

INTERVIEWER: How did the play strike you when you first read it?

PETER HALL: I remember having received the script of *The Homecoming* through the post with a letter from Harold Pinter saying: "Dear Peter, here it is. Yours ever. . . ." I mention that because I think it's important. What it was was what it was. And although my views of it changed in emphasis as we worked, it seemed to me such a complete play on first reading and my responses changed very little. I think during our working time we cut maybe twelve or fifteen lines, not more. The play was there as a complete thing in its own right. I thought at the time it came that this play looks unblinkingly at life in the human jungle. It's not a pleasant play. It's not a play which is comfortable. It's abrasive and uncomfortable.

INTERVIEWER: Did the jungle image occur to you right away?

HALL: Yes, right away. There's something deeply animalistic about the people's reactions to each other and the way they treat each other. So if we want a word, that was my reaction. A jungle. I remember Harold had warned me. All he'd said about the play was, "I'm writing a play about a man coming home who's secretly married; and it's going to be quite something. And it's going to present you with great difficulties." Because it came to me just after we'd done *Marat/Sade* and *Afore Night Come*—and there'd been a great scream from a minority of people in London about us doing dirty plays—Harold had warned me jokingly that another piece of dirt was arriving.

9

I did not classify it or the other plays as "dirt." I merely warned my board that the controversy might continue. It didn't.

I must explain that when I read a play, I read it straight through. I've always found that at the end of that one reading I know whether I ought to direct it or not. I couldn't for the life of me at the end of a first reading be interviewed and say what it was about or *why* I wanted to direct it. But I know whether I can do it or not. And one has to trust the instinct in this way, because if I finish a play and think, "Well I don't think so," and read it a second, third, fourth, fifth, sixth time—by the sixth time, I bet you any money that I'll be directing it, because I see that there are problems that will be interesting to solve . . . that is if it's of any standard at all. I get fascinated by how to get over the problems. So I have to have just that first reading. And I didn't then study *The Homecoming* very closely. I just knew I had to do it.

INTERVIEWER: Did you arrive at any conceptual idea of the play before starting rehearsal?

HALL: I read the text so often that I more or less knew it by heart. I'd also worked hard with John Bury [the designer] and with Harold Pinter on what the thing should look like. Pinter wrote this play for the Aldwych and he says in his stage directions, "A large room." This is partly because we'd worked together on two of his other plays at the Aldwych and he'd been rather preoccupied, and rightly, by the fact that the Aldwych is a very large stage. And he said to me, "I think properly speaking that this is a large play that needs a large room, and it'll go on a large stage." His stage directions are minimal—I think any good playwright's are—if you can't pick up what it's like and where it is and what the whole tone of the thing is about from actually reading the text, then no amount of descriptive passages are going to help you. I suppose before we started I had a set which was simple, antiseptic, gray, dead—I mean it reminded me of an old butcher who used to be covered in blood and is now in a sterile world.

INTERVIEWER: You accept Max's biographical credentials?

HALL: Yes, I take him on trust as an old butcher. I would, though, hesitate to argue with you if you said he isn't a butcher —for purposes of this discussion, he is butcher enough. It's a sterile world from which women have been excluded; the set has to mirror that.

This is my process of work before I begin rehearsal: I jot down every physical or atmospheric thing that I pick up from the text which seems worth exploring in the design. I can't remember how I briefed John Bury, but I would certainly have talked about the antiseptic and the sterile, the unfeminine.

INTERVIEWER: The impression of the set was monumental.

HALL: Yes. That was part of Pinter's idea. Because the back wall has been knocked down "to make an open living area." Within this place of horror a larger space has been made, an emptier space for the figures to confront each other in. "Living area" is an ironic term for this jungle. Although one begins to work with the designer and tries all sorts of ways of mirroring the actual function of the play, more than anything else I think you have to have a subjective image of what kind of play it is and what impression, what atmosphere you want to create, and make sure that that is secure enough so that the set doesn't contradict it as you work. One of the most ghastly things in the theater is designing the set before you begin rehearsals. In an ideal world I would like to work with the actors for a month and then design the production. But that never happens except with the Berliner Ensemble where they have enormous rehearsal time. In this case, though, I knew my Pinter, I already had a close working relationship with him, and I liked very much his form of theater. Pinter's ambiguity in technical terms is that he makes silence speak by defining silence by the noise around it. He equally well makes movements and action unbearably meaningful by the stillness on either side of them. Therefore a Pinter set has to be stripped to its absolute essential so that a movement means the thing it ought to mean. You can't litter a Pinter set, or Pinter staging, or Pinter performances with any kind of naturalism that tries to kid the audience that they're not in a theater. So certainly my brief to John Bury—this I do remember—said, "We will have nothing on the stage except what is necessary," because what is necessary will speak that much more eloquently. So we took everything away except a few pieces of furniture.

INTERVIEWER: Is there any special relationship between character and environment in *The Homecoming*?

HALL: I think all of Harold's work relates to a confined space where people confront each other in often very ugly terms. Territorial rights? It hadn't occurred to me. But it's patriarchal with the boss figure, and everyone's trying to castrate the boss in one way or another. So certainly I would accept this, after the event, as part of an analysis. You see, in everything I say I want to emphasize this very very strongly. Harold always refuses to say what his plays *mean*, and I think quite rightly. I don't think one can literally define metaphor. A metaphor reverberates and has many meanings to many people, and that's why it's a metaphor. In the same way I don't think I as a director can say why I consciously did this or that, because I don't work like that. I can only tell you, as far as I can remember, what the processes were behind it, but I didn't sit in a corner and say, Jungle—therefore the linoleum should have green tones in it. Or, Space —therefore let's put the walls like this. Perhaps half the time I couldn't have explained in my work with John Bury why we were going in the direction we were. And I remember the first model we presented to Pinter—I remember him being very concerned about the pillar that ran across the top of the set, which is where the wall had been knocked down. In our first model it was very rough hewn; it was very obvious that a wall had been knocked down, and a large beam had been put in to keep the house up. Harold quite rightly said, "Yes, that's right, but it's too explicit." When they talk about the wall being knocked down and the audience looks, *then* they should understand why the wall is like it is; but when the curtain goes up they shouldn't look and say, "Ah, a wall has been knocked down and a beam has been put in."

Perhaps this is a suitable moment for saying how I work with Pinter. We had and still have a very close working relationship and I think our terms of reference are very clear. He can say whatever he likes to me about the way I'm directing his play, but I remain the final arbiter of what is done in the production. And I can say whatever I like about his text, but he remains the final arbiter of what is in and what is out. That sounds very simple, and it's always worked with us over quite a long and complex period. And we said those things equally to each other *in front of the cast*, which is enough to make some actors run screaming from the theater. But in this case, it didn't. We had six actors who had a sufficiently rich relationship with each other and with us for it to be a totally acceptable working form. So we were able to be quite frank, and I think this is terribly important. If an actor's not big enough to be told why he's doing it wrongly, or a dramatist's not big enough to be told why the line is not working, or a director's not big enough to be told that the scene is all wrong, then nothing can actually come out. I don't believe in pride in the theater. But you can only collaborate in this way when everybody is secure. Which means working in a company. And this is precisely how I tried to make the Royal Shakespeare Company.

I think why Harold and I have worked well together is that finally we do coalesce into one person in terms of the production. We have a complete reaction on each other. So if you said to me, "Could you have done that production without Harold Pinter?" I would certainly say, "No, I couldn't." I would have done a production which would have been in some ways very similar, but it wouldn't have been like that. And I think he would say exactly the same. But he didn't direct it, and I didn't write it.

INTERVIEWER: Did you work on *The Homecoming* with the same musical values that apply to his previous plays?

HALL: Ultimately yes. But musical values only come from meaning. What did impress me about the play was its ugly brutality. I think that the writing is as meticulous and formed as ever. But underneath the writing there is a pressure of emotion and an ugliness of motive which I think is a new note in his work—because he's dealt in the past with menace and with violence, but in a rather cool and sophisticated way. In this play there seemed to be something unleashed which gave the work to me—and I choose my words very carefully—brutal and epic proportions. I think this is the biggest play he's written. It has the largest size; it's the most painful, and deals with the rawest emotions; although it continues to express them for a lot of the time in terms of ambiguity and mockery. The phrase always on our lips when we were doing this play was "Taking the piss." It's a cockney phrase meaning getting the better of your opponent by mockery. This play doesn't take the piss in a light or flippant way. It takes the piss in a cruel and bitter way. The characters are all doing this to each other. They take the piss—this cockneyism is central to the play. But of course one of the great factors about taking the piss is that if you're taking the piss satisfactorily the person whose piss is being taken must not be sure whether or not it is being taken! And this was the first problem for the actors.

I always like to present actors at the beginning of rehearsals with an image we can refer to later. It may be modified—it must be modified, and will change—but in general, I try to state why I want to do the play and what it's about without being over-literal. In this sense I did talk about the jungle and destructiveness and the unfeminine society, the hatred of women which informs this society. The resentment of the male animal, that he is born of woman and needs woman in order to create more people. But I didn't give them a sentence which said "This is what the play *says*."

INTERVIEWER: How did the two absent figures of MacGregor and the dead wife color the production?

HALL: We talked about them a great deal. In our work they were living characters. We gradually knew what kind of a bastard MacGregor was, and what kind of a rapacious bitchlike lady

Jessie was. But these two figures only colored the production in relation to each character's views of them. If you said to me now, "What was MacGregor like?" I could only tell you what he or she was like to the person in the play that I was discussing it with. And there are certain contradictions, because Pinter is writing a play that takes cognizance of the fact that everybody's view of everybody else is slightly different and that there are many more than two sides to every question.

In the early stages of the work we always circumscribed ourselves by saying, "Let's not move physically in the staging at all unless it's absolutely necessary." Perhaps I can expand that a little bit more. In the early stages of work, when an actor is still learning his lines and still exploring motives, there is a great tendency to move around the stage or to physicalize motives as an alibi, for want of something better to do. In the old days you always went and took a drink from the cocktail cabinet or you lit a cigarette. I think that Pinter's concentrated form of theater means that *nothing* must happen on the stage when it is not relevant, *ever*. If a man lights a cigarette it mustn't just be that he happens to light a cigarette. It's got to contribute.

So I encouraged the actors in this very sparse, spare unfurnished room just to sit around and talk to each other and not to try and move. But at the same time we explored all kinds of naturalistic behavior, naturalistic motives. In Pinter, as in Beckett, you need to start with naturalistic exploration. And the process would apply to another great stylist, Edward Albee. You should examine all the naturalistic motives only for one reason: Pinter (or Beckett) is a highly formed and in my view poetic dramatist, and the actor's task is already heavily circumscribed. He can only say what is written, and not an approximation. Therefore he has an exterior formula given to him, a very highly stylized form of utterance, even. And unless you give him the rein to naturalize it and let free his own emotions and instincts, it could be a puppetlike performance. I was very aware of this in *The Homecoming*, and I think, if I may say so, one of the achievements of the production is that it sailed dangerously near to a puppetlike production without being one. And out of that tension was born what I believe it had to be.

I think that is true of any poetic drama. That was the main stylistic task. I made them learn the lines with meticulous accuracy. And it's not generally, perhaps, understood, how slovenly actors are about text. A lot of the texts they work on are so imprecise that the actors might just as well be slovenly; an "and" instead of a "but" doesn't make much difference. In Shakespeare it's amazing what gets by because actors learn lazily and they *have* to learn meticulously. I think the problem is exactly like that of an opera singer. No opera singer would think of not learning a Mozart aria with the most meticulous regard for the notes. The problem of then making them true and human is a later problem. And that's what we did with *The Homecoming*. I not only asked them to learn the words, but I asked them to be absolutely aware of Harold's shorthand. He has this technique (which again he shares with Sam Beckett): If there is a pause in the proceedings, for a small pause he puts three dots; for a large pause he puts "Pause"; for a very, very long pause he puts "Silence." Now of course it's not just enough to do that; because you have to *fill* those indications. But if one analyzes the scene, every time one of those three things happens there is a bridge which dramatists of the past have always verbalized. Now, Harold writes in silence as much as he does in words; he defines silence by the noise on either side of it and the literal communication on either side of it. So you have to discover what goes on through that. It's very easy in learning to miss this. And if as a director one doesn't keep one's eye on the text during rehearsal all the time, you forget that Harold has said, "There is a bridge here which you've got to find." Remember, Shakespeare only used silence this way once. Coriolanus answers his mother's great plea not to burn Rome with a stage direction: "Holds her by the hand, silent."

INTERVIEWER: Did you hold special rehearsals for silences?

HALL: I did once have a dot and pause rehearsal. It drove

the actors absolutely mad. I said, "You don't remember the phrases." Exactly as if an actor in Shakespeare had learned his text without knowing where the ends of the lines are, which is the whole phrasing unit. If you run the line on in Shakespeare, which you must once in ten, you still must *know* where the end of the line is. So I said, "We will now sit down and have a word rehearsal, sitting where we are, and each of you will tell me where your dots are and where your pauses are and where your silences are." And we went right through it. It only happened once. It was just to try and make the actors understand that we were dealing with something which was highly formed and highly wrought. And our first responsibility was to know what it was.

INTERVIEWER: Was there any metrical timing?

HALL: No. That would be like conducting a piece of music with a metronome. I wouldn't do that with Shakespeare either. In the case of a concert, the rehearsed phrasing happens slightly differently because of the human dynamic of the conductor. In the case of a theater performance, the phrasing which has been set happens slightly differently because of the actor and the audience response. And any attempt to say, "Hold this for four seconds" is as bad as saying to an actor, "Walk four steps to the left or four steps to the right," which I would never do. I think people who hear that I held a dot and pause rehearsal perhaps misunderstand its purpose. It wasn't done to imprison the actor, but to add to his knowledge of the text.

But after the period of naturalistic exploration we took away everything which didn't relate. And who was the arbiter of that? Well, me—with Harold at my side making comments when he wanted. I seem to remember in the early days there was much more carry-on with Joey coming home with his coat and his boxing bag, much more naturalism, and all he had to do was come in with his bag and stand still. I seem to remember that there was a great deal more cigarette smoking on the part of Max to keep him comfortable sitting in that central chair. I remember that there was a lot more walking around the room, particularly on the part of Sam the chauffeur-brother. And gradually we whittled these away to give the thing a kind of strength, so that a move was a positive shock. Or the glass of water was an object, which was horrifyingly real because it was so isolated. And that was a very difficult time for the actors because all their props were removed.

INTERVIEWER: How far were actors allowed to rely on given biography?

HALL: Completely, unless there is textual evidence that there are two sides to the question. The given biographies are used during the first process of naturalistic exploration. For instance, what does Joey the construction man feel like coming home to go straight down to the gym? We decided all sorts of things: that Joey, having to keep up as a boxer and all the rest was pretty shagged out most of the time. But finally that wasn't at all significant; it didn't mean anything. It's the kind of thing that we explored and cast aside. Didn't help. I think in the selecting stage that it is extremely hard, and important in Pinter, to try and keep every situation open ended. I *did* say to the company that the play was like a diamond which presented many facets to an audience. Well, what the actors had to do was not select a facet to be presented, but to show many facets at once. So that it was almost like something being moved around. But it always had to be logical to the actor himself from moment to moment. And of course one of the fatal things to do in that jungle is to be honest or to be candid or sincere, because if you do you immediately become vulnerable. The characters destroy any sign of actual truth in each other. It was very hard indeed to find a coherence which an audience could understand. And as you know, some people didn't. Maybe they thought too much instead of feeling it.

INTERVIEWER: Was there any attempt to implant any unspoken sense of what the characters really want?

HALL: No, because I think that the play is so complex that to give any simple solution really reduces it to an anecdote. You have to see it from each character's point of view, and they all judge it differently, in different terms; you have to shift from one to another and see how it works for each of them in turn. Gradually you piece together this very complicated structure, and I found the play's complexity as it moved toward its end of rehearsals, grew greater. It was clearer, yet *more* complex.

INTERVIEWER: Is it part of the director's job to resolve ambiguities?

HALL: In the case of Harold Pinter it's not his job at all. It is his job to present the contradictions clearly. Also I think worthwhile theater always deals in ambiguity. The only kind of theater that's really interesting is something which is, in the proper sense of the term, poetic, which is produced by the clash of opposites and reverberates beyond its literal meaning. Well, if you say, I've got an interpretation of *The Homecoming*—and many were advanced to me, as they were years ago about *Godot* when I did it—you then have a simple literal meaning which is not a metaphor.

INTERVIEWER: What about the production groupings? For instance, when Max hits Joey, is this something you consciously attempted?

HALL: I didn't think anything as we did them. I did not say, "Let's do that because it will show. . . ." I built it up as a situation and it seemed inevitable finally. It went through many stages before it did seem inevitable. There were many times when it went wrong. I don't think you consciously think up a bit of business to express something. Business evolves, you suggest certain things, you create an atmosphere in which the actors create something with you, and you then relate that to your central instinct about the play and either discard it or keep it. I think it's for other people to say, "That expressed this for me." I do remember many years ago Harold Hobson [*Sunday Times* of London] writing a long piece about a moment of Christian clarification in *Godot* when Vladimir took off his hat and said, "Christ have mercy upon us." That, quite rightly, had not been in any of our minds when we did it; the actor had wanted to take his hat off. It seemed to me the right place. I'm not saying that Harold Hobson was wrong, but it wasn't in our minds when we did it. And I think if it *had* been in our minds, everybody would have found it acutely embarrassing and literal.

INTERVIEWER: Was the stylistic finesse of the production (e.g., the cigarette-lighting group opening up like a flower) an answer to the brutality of the material? The more brutal the contents, the finer the shell?

HALL: That's not my solution to Pinter; that's Pinter's solution to Pinter. The bestiality of the play is encased in the very elegant shell of the writing, which is extremely meticulous, formed, and rhythmic, and certainly has—in some areas you've mentioned, I agree—a vigor and crudity which is a new quality in him; but it still has this extraordinary finesse. Harold Pinter's style as a playwright led me to do the things I did in physical form. This production was a culmination of the experiences we'd had together.

INTERVIEWER: What was the reason for the Teddy change in America?

HALL: Teddy was only changed because Michael Bryant, who played it in England, couldn't go. So we got Michael Craig to play it. A new personality brought new problems and new qualities, which was good. I think it was actually a great help to the production—to the other five—that there was a new factor. I can't compare the two performances; I thought they were both brilliant. Michael Bryant was so much the campus intellectual who'd opted out of any kind of responsibility in human terms, wanted to keep his hands clean. He did that absolutely beautifully. Michael Craig got some of that, but he also had something else which in some ways made the play even more horrific. He was the biggest bastard of the lot, as well as being the withdrawn intellectual. He really was. So when he went at the end, leaving his wife, he was not in any way a victim or a martyr. He was the biggest shit of all. He was leaving them with their deserts. He was leaving her with her deserts. And he was the worst of the lot.

INTERVIEWER: At what point does the production indicate Teddy's decision to abandon her?

HALL: I think he brings her back—now I am intellectualizing, which I didn't do until after I'd done the play—he brings his wife back to the jungle to have her tested by the laws of the jungle, and makes one vow: that he will not lift a finger to alter the outcome of the test, one way or the other.

INTERVIEWER: Is Teddy still a part of the jungle himself?

HALL: He's produced by the jungle, so this is the necessary place he must bring his wife to. But I don't think he goes out a defeated man, or a saddened man, or a martyred man. He goes back, in a way, confirmed in the family's hatred of women. In that sense, he's victorious. Because Lenny can't break him. Joey actually having his wife can't break him. He apparently is unbreakable. And if she wants to stay, she can stay. But of course he plays it all so cool it could look as though he doesn't care at all. He does care, but he's not going to be involved in any action about that caring.

If I had made the speech I have just made to you about Teddy to the actor playing Teddy, I think he would have been incapable of playing the last scene. Because he would have had a very crude and simple objective, which is, I'm not going to lift a finger to do anything about this. And it is much more complex than that, because Teddy's motives change almost from second to second. The amount of force he has to apply to keeping uninvolved—that's the main thing, and that I would discuss with the actor: How do you manage to sit there, how? Can you imagine this situation? How can you keep control? But you mustn't ever produce an actor by giving him the results, because then he acts results. You can ask him the right questions. You can hint at a path he can follow. You can't tell him what the audience should see. I suppose I could have said what I've said about Teddy while I was doing the play to an outsider, but I wouldn't have it said to the actor. One can only go on what is said in the text. When you're dealing with Pinter, you're not dealing with seven types of ambiguity, but an infinite number of ambiguities. Because any proposition we draw from one side of the play we can contradict or modify by a proposition from some other side.

INTERVIEWER: Are there any types of human material which an actor could legitimately bring to another playwright but not to Pinter?

HALL: An actor must bring his own instincts and his own responses to any play. Paul Rogers certainly brought to Max his understanding of aggression; all the ideas of a family life being an opportunity to release aggression; the hatred of his sons because they were younger than him. Each one of the actors drew on themselves. They always must. And the background, I think, is terribly important: the building site, the pimp, the intellectual, the campus figure, that girl who was some kind of call-girl or model, or was she? These have to be investigated and lived and understood by the actor; they have to bring the problem to themselves, because otherwise one would get an entirely arid experience. I would say that the personal involvement of the actor in Pinter has to be deeper and more passionate and more instinctive at a certain time in rehearsal, and then one has to cool it. In the jungle it is dangerous to show one's feelings. The process still goes on. But we had some rehearsals in which we tried to explore the dangers. We didn't have improvisations as such, but we did say: Actor A—If you see an opening, a vulnerability, a commitment, a sincerity, anything that you could get back on in the other man, say it. So that everyone was *guarded*. And this really raised the whole thing to fever pitch. What I'm saying is that all the characters are feeling passionate, ugly, instinctive, destructive, and they can't even show those things. To shout in that house is a weakness. You have to contain everything. Now the minute the actors started to say, "Well if we're going to contain everything, hide everything, then why bother to feel it?" the play went dead. So it was a passionate and violent and instinctive exercise for them in which their fellow actors on the stage had to be used as people from whom they hid these feelings; but they had to undergo them at each performance. Otherwise it became pastel and totally enigmatic. So the part played by the instinct of the actor, I think, is greater in a way because Pinter is a very passionate dramatist in that sense and *demands* passion from his actor. And if you just play the surface of Pinter it is apparently incoherent. One has seen productions of Pinter where the actors just said the words, or naturalized them, and they don't mean anything at all.

INTERVIEWER: What about the rehearsal period?

HALL: We rehearsed it for six weeks, which was our normal period at that time. We went on tour though and worked on it a bit on tour; then we worked on it again before we took it to New York. Walter Kerr didn't like it, and at that point New York's opinion of a play was apparently only his. Alexander Cohen, who'd brought us over, said, "You'll be off in a fortnight." I said, "Is that a definite promise, because I need these actors at home." And he was very cross. They say it doesn't matter if you succeed or fail; but in fact there's still this belief on Broadway that if you fail you ought to feel punished. But then he fought for the play and it won all the Tony awards and became a great success. I do appreciate the fight he made for the play, which made it a success. I think the production was at its best in New York; by that time, it had really been fined down to a cutting edge.

INTERVIEWER: In what areas is Pinter most flexible as a collaborator?

HALL: He's an actor, and a director, and a man of the theater: I think he's extremely flexible. He has his opinions, and so he bloody well should with the genius he's got. But he respects other people's opinions and is never arbitrary. As a director, if you question a scene or a speech or a word, he never *collects* his genius around him like a protective cloak and says, "That's my business." He is open. That's all I can say. He's entirely flexible; finally, if he's in the right and believes he's in the right, he says he's in the right; and it's my job as the director to bow to him. Actually I don't remember that there was an author dispute or a director dispute left on the stage by the time we'd finished.

INTERVIEWER: Will you tell me more about the set?

HALL: The set took its final form before we began rehearsals. But the exact placement of the furniture and exactly *what* it was, did not. I remember I staged the first scene in a totally different way to begin with; then I changed it and it stayed the way it is now.

INTERVIEWER: What about the images, Lenny on the threshold, etc.?

HALL: Yes. I never said to Ian Holm, "Lenny's always on the threshold, let's see if we can work that in." It's just that in our investigation of the play, Lenny was often on the threshold. I can see it now . . . the images were arrived at by work. If you give an actor a move, it's no good. If the process of work dictates the move, it's a good move. I think this is where Pinter's stage directions are splendid, because they leave open the investigation of these things. As soon as a dramatist says, "Max hits Sam across the head with an upraised stick, having the air of a man who is frustrated," the actor reads that, the director reads that, well, that's it! Finish! It'll never express that; it won't even express what's been described. Pinter never makes that mistake.

In a lot of the appreciations of the production there was a lot of talk about its stylistic qualities, that it had a stylized form. I would just like to make clear that it wasn't a conscious decision before the work was done, and it wasn't a style that I was aiming at, because I don't think one can work that way. I don't know what my style is; that's for other people to say, if I have one. Anyway, my style has to be altered, changed, modified by the dictates of the particular play. So the style was dictated very much by the play, I hope, and is produced by the work process. Style is doing within the premise of the play. I am very much in sympathy with the idea of doing nothing and having nothing on the stage unless it means something; but there are other plays that one can think of which require a great deal of naturalistic bolstering—obviously the plays of the naturalistic revolution which you have to think of, at least at first, in those terms. But it wasn't a stylistic exercise, this production. And I think, thanks to Pinter the playwright and his collaboration with me as a director, it's one of the few productions I've done in my life in which what was on the stage, if I may say this, was better than my first concept of it. I think that's happened to me four times in my life, and usually it's the other way round.

INTERVIEWER: Is that the benefit of working with your own company?

HALL: Absolutely. I could not have put an ad hoc group through that needling and meticulous process. They would have felt that they were in corsets.

—INTERVIEWED BY IRVING WARDLE

A DESIGNER'S APPROACH

An Interview with John Bury

INTERVIEWER: Your set melded so closely with the play that it was not a painted backdrop, but part of the play. If you can take Pinter at his word, his feelings about the space of a stage, then the room is as a microcosm.

JOHN BURY: There was never a moment where we sat down and said, "What does it mean?" Harold asked for a room where a back wall had been knocked down to show a staircase in the hall. He didn't specify that it should be large or small, or gray or white. This was purely a physical requirement of the text. Harold has, in the past, shown a complete abhorrence of the composite set. He hated *The Birthday Party* on a composite set. He hates composite sets because, I think, he feels that there has to be a good reality in the room. Once the theater man starts giving you cut-away walls, staircases, screens, and front doors, you get a composite set. This is the designer's answer to those wretched people who write plays all over the place, because you get so many television writers in the theater now who think a theater can do anything because Shakespeare did everything. They don't understand or even study stage conventions, so they write their *Five Finger Exercises*, with a bedroom, a living room, and a loo [toilet] on stage. This really isn't valid, because you can't do anything except build a composite set. But if you get a good director, who's strong enough, he rewrites the thing and puts it into a tunnel. When Harold wanted to produce this play—which demanded in fact, a composite set because he wanted to see the hall, the front door, and the staircase—he got around this by writing into the text that line about knocking the wall down to make an open living area. Instead of a composite set becoming a stage device, which let the audience look through very careful angles to see the staircase and the room, he made it a single living area.

INTERVIEWER: So that line was a technical device rather than a theme within the play?

BURY: My feeling is that this is how Harold justified to himself the use of that set. He thought, "Christ, I can't have a composite set. This is quite simple: Teddy can say that line, then the whole thing falls into place." Then what I had to do was to make it absolutely clear. My early versions tended to make the whole thing look like a modern composite living area —a design of an archway through into the hall. That worried us.

INTERVIEWER: Why did it worry you?

BURY: It didn't quite jell. It was too clean, too tidy. So Peter [Hall] said, "What in fact do the beams do?" And I said, "If you knock a wall down, you have to put in a couple of big piers and put a RSG [rigid steel girder] across it. You can't just knock a wall down, else it caves in. You have to put the beams in first." He said, "Suppose we take the situation as the boys did it, but they didn't get any further." We had a big Victorian room in which someone has built two brick piers and put in a RSG. So then I built a model and literally did that, where the brick and the RSG weren't in fact melded in. This Harold felt was too crude, too strong, and turned it into a play about a room with a RSG and brick piers. But I said that this was obviously the right thing, let's just soften it. So I plastered and painted it, but so that you could still see the RSG. You could see the steelwork and the difference of texture between the two piers as being whitewashed brick as opposed to wallpaper in the rest of the house.

INTERVIEWER: Did Pinter lavish a lot of attention on the set? Did he demand things besides the obvious things which were in the text?

BURY: He was interested in the total feel, but he didn't bother me about details. He's not the sort who chases a designer around.

INTERVIEWER: He seems to me, more than most playwrights, conscious of using a set, as opposed to just having it there.

BURY: That's right. One must get the right sort of criticism, a designer can't work on his own. He needs someone to bounce off. If you get the right sort of director and the right sort of author, like Hall and Pinter, they help in terms of what the set means to them. Like Harold saying that he can't let the set make it a play about a beam. That it was too dominant. He didn't say, "I think that's a bit high, or that's a bit low, or that's the wrong color, or the set should be bigger."

INTERVIEWER: Did he want the set to evoke certain emotions, so that certain colors would throw that off?

BURY: I wasn't given any clue to the color scheme. My first model Peter and Harold accepted straight away. There are certain things in the set, which when you first sit down, you do. Certain statements that are yours about the play and they're usually the right ones, and you don't want to change anything. I made about four models, but certain things were right from the start—like I didn't like the color scheme. One just had to work with Hall on things like furniture layout.

INTERVIEWER: Can I ask you about furniture layout? In the printed text it seems very explicit. Was it explicit in the script?

BURY: No, it was clear that Max had an armchair, I think. That's really about all.

INTERVIEWER: And then you just acquired the furniture as you went along?

BURY: We worked out roughly what we needed. The broken-down sofa referred to in the text we turned it into a couch because we had problems. Basically Peter evolved that set-up, working through the model.

INTERVIEWER: You just dropped in things and they added or subtracted?

BURY: Peter did this, I don't think Harold did. We scaled the furniture to the layout, and I don't think that during rehearsal we changed anything.

INTERVIEWER: If you look at the objects you get an eerie feeling that they have a life of their own and are tipped at angles that are revealing.

BURY: Yes, this is the second stage of design. One hopes that in any play nothing should go on stage that isn't valid and doesn't have a meaning. When one has got rid of one's director and one's actors and done the design and got the furniture plotted, this is when the designer comes into his own, because he can take his chairs away and choose his cushions and his fabrics and his paints. You don't have to be answerable right through rehearsals. Otherwise you would become a kind of stage manager.

INTERVIEWER: The interesting thing about the space, at least in the New York production, was that you were not aware until the play developed of the superlarge, of the surreal. Is that something that you were working for?

BURY: Yes, but it's also one's feeling about what theater is. The stage has to balance the auditorium, the actors, and the sightlines. What makes so many sets look dreary and dinky is that they don't fit the theater. The set here was designed to fit the theater exactly. The proscenium arch, the walls and the auditorium were all one space. This is what one can always do in repertory because one's designing for a particular stage. But in the commercial stage, you don't know what theater you're going into when you build. This set wouldn't have any classic dignity if it were placed on a stage the wrong shape for it. So the supersize of the set in New York came, to a certain extent, from the fact that you had the width on the stage.

INTERVIEWER: This to my mind added something. When the curtain came up, you said, "This is a room, it's very conventional!" And suddenly it became bigger, which I thought was marvelous. Was it intended that way?

BURY: One knew it was big, what one didn't want was for

the walls to disappear. We tend to work in a box because we're all proscenium, the Aldwych stage ends there. And you want to make this room fit round this proscenium. Once one starts making a great set-up which doesn't match the theater, it becomes self-conscious. It sort of says, "Look at me."

INTERVIEWER: Something that amazed me about your set was that it absolutely meshed with the play and when you discovered the set, you discovered it late in the show.

BURY: You're right there. This is something one was after, as with any set, really. We specialize in what we call "gray box design." We have now realized our whole thesis of using the stage as an acting area in relationship to the audience, without impeding decoration. And nowadays, nearly all our work is done on the gray box which balances with the auditorium, and just those elements which you actually need are put into a gray box. These are usually mobile elements, because for Shakespeare you don't have a unit which is there for the whole play, except possibly the floor.

INTERVIEWER: The beam and the staircase took on a strength, phallic, and almost manneristic. Was that something you felt when you designed it?

BURY: Yes, this is part of all my work, which tends to be over-large and over-heavy.

INTERVIEWER: I think it's a positive asset.

BURY: Yes, what one attempts to do is get an immense feeling of weight on stage.

INTERVIEWER: Do you mean an almost sexual energy?

BURY: I don't know that it need be sexual. You said mannerist, which is not necessarily sexual at all. Mannerism does creep in a lot. But I don't think there was anything sexual, phallic.

INTERVIEWER: The environment seemed so swollen.

BURY: The environment is essentially masculine. That was the whole point about that house. There wasn't anything feminine about it. That set couldn't be dirty. It wasn't squalid, because of the reference to cleanliness. Those men cleaned that place out of existence. Washed and wiped up their tea cups. It wasn't *The Caretaker*. It wasn't dust and grubbiness. But it was essentially faded, like a carpet that had been beaten, wallpaper that had never been changed. The corners were a bit frayed. It was a house no feminine hand ever entered, no one ever put a bit of chintz on a cushion, no one ever arranged the flowers in a vase. It was barracklike. This came out of the play. But it was difficult to get this degree of sordidness without being dirty. One couldn't actually have hanging-off paper and one couldn't actually have dirty corners. When designing *The Caretaker* one could just show litter. But with this one, it's got to be clean—the butcher's shop.

INTERVIEWER: Very strong and scrubbed. And with the meat, there is such a fantastic sexuality in that job, and yet this has the strength without the juice.

BURY: Yes, this is the mark a designer works along. It shouldn't be me saying this is my idea of a phallic staircase.

INTERVIEWER: I wondered if you considered that when you did it?

BURY: No, I don't think so. One tries as far as possible to work in the subconscious. A lot of work in a set is never even talked about. I don't think we discussed our reasons for the color scheme or the floor. It was done and they said "Yes, that's right." But we talked about where a chair should go and whether a beam should be covered, and how much room we needed at the back of the set on stage; the sightlines or the problems of looking out of the window onto the street. Was it necessary to bring a window into a sightline? This is where you need the cooperation of the director and the author. You get people who are not competent about stage dialogue who say all he's got to do is pull the curtains and look out onto the street, and a West End or Broadway management would say that the window had to be in sightline. One used to have stipulations that all exits and entrances should be in full sightline. This is because an actor wanted to do an exit line, and if you gave him a room with an area not in full sightline, he couldn't go to the door and do his exit line and get his applause. In *The Homecoming*, the window was out, so was the bottom of the staircase and the point they looked at the door. Again the non-use of the door, I think, made the door far more real than if you had a stage door. The moment you get a stage door, which clunks and bangs, it doesn't work.

INTERVIEWER: The fact that it wasn't there makes the room much more like a cage, in the sense that you can't get out.

BURY: In fact it was there, it was a great huge door which the actors walked through and banged and had a key to. The audience believed the door was there. It's always been one of my credos that stage doors weren't just doors because they would shudder and bang. You know the feeling about a stage door. But if you can have the door in an alcove and make the actors work it, everybody believes the door's there, far more than seeing it. And the same with that window. They went to a window and opened the curtains and they had to stand back and speak the line. This is something which a lesser director would not let you do. He'd say that window's got to be in sightline because of the actor's business at it. But the whole point and quality of the set is destroyed by making this sort of demand on the designer.

INTERVIEWER: In America your set seemed claustrophobic. That room was large, but it nonetheless seemed small to the extent that it was heavy and massive and bore in on the family.

BURY: This was because it was a claustrophobic theater.

INTERVIEWER: This was not an unconscious choice of yours for a massive, monumental, but concentrated area in center stage?

BURY: Not essentially. This was more or less dictated by the theater, because you can't simply impose on a theater, you have to use the space. In spatial terms, you can't turn the Aldwych into the Playbox.

INTERVIEWER: You said that Pinter treats the designer like

he treats the actors, he doesn't tell them much. He lets them find the play. Have you attempted to ask him things, or is it merely understood that those are his rules?

BURY: Yes, he doesn't know and will admit he doesn't know.

INTERVIEWER: He just waits for things to jell?

BURY: Yes, he won't tell you about the mother, you're left to find out from the play. One day Harold will say he thinks this, and on another day he thinks something else.

INTERVIEWER: Which is just as valid.

BURY: Yes. I think he was writing a play one day about two boys, and the next day he said, "I've discovered they're sisters." And I remember one of the cast saying, "I can't understand it, he's writing a play, he can make them brothers or sisters. What does it mean, he's not discovered whether they're boys or girls?" This is obviously someone who has no knowledge of Harold's creative process. We all discover things. I discover it with a set. One doesn't know what one is going to build until one starts the model. Harold is an example, par excellence, of the creative process. He won't tell you what happened—to Lenny, to the mother.

INTERVIEWER: Nor should he. What interests me are his suggestions. One is not interested in specifics, but in the texture of the imagination.

BURY: This absolutely throws out the whole of the Stanislavski school of production and acting. Under the old rule you all sit down and you decide. And you decide imaginatively a set of given circumstances. You invent your granny and your mother and your whole life history, and everybody's got to know the mother and everybody's got to agree to the same image of mother. Then when you all act, you'll put mother on stage. And usually with Stanislavski one's working with a dead author or a translation, so you and the director have to establish a given set of circumstances. This is the thing with Harold—there are no given circumstances. You don't get a common image. Harold is particular in his talent. He doesn't represent a summation of a school. There's lots of imitation Pinter, but I think he's very individual in his work. It is his quality of language that interests one, and imagination. As a designer, one is very consciously leaving the air clear for the imagination to work. One is deliberately trying to create an atmosphere where anything could happen. One knows this and one isn't trying to put one's own thesis across. One is constantly taking away and refining and abstracting.

—INTERVIEWED BY JOHN LAHR

THE TERRITORIAL STRUGGLE

Irving Wardle

Dramatists are not original philosophers, but the great ages of drama generally roll in an idea: some blueprint of the nature of Man from which the dramatist constructs a working model to be tested for its all-round performance and behavior under stress.

For Elizabethans encountering the Machiavellian malcontent or for Mrs. Aphra Behn's audiences encountering the noble savage, there can hardly have been much difficulty in relating the dramatic character to its philosophic prototype. Similarly in our century we usually know whose progeny we are seeing on the stage: Freudian Man, Marxist Man, or the Absurdist issue of Existential Man. However, when Harold Pinter's characters first appeared in public in 1958, nobody knew who the father was—and Pinter certainly wasn't telling.

For critics, more than for other people, this is an inconvenience. Before you can say anything with any confidence, you feel you have to get the ideological coordinates right. Who was Stanley in *The Birthday Party*? A helpless ego, engaging in polymorphous infant games with a mother substitute until the cruel super-ego intervenes in the person of Goldberg? Or an economic nebbish, who falls victim to the capitalist forces of business and state religion?

It didn't add up. Nor did Arnold Wesker's complaint that Pinter had willfully disguised what should have been a straightforward fable about the Jewish community. We all dug around and discovered Pinter liked Kafka, and Beckett, and American gangster films, and I, for one, came up with the phrase "comedy of menace" which explained nothing but at least supplied a comforting label.

Then came *The Caretaker* and we were in trouble again. The menace was still there, but so were qualities that looked disturbingly like kindness and generosity. Kenneth Tynan, as I recall, ranked Pinter with Van Gogh as the owner of one of history's most notable ears, and called the play a dialogue between the super-ego and the id. Elsewhere it was described as an investigation of human charity.

Five years later when *The Homecoming* opened at the Aldwych Theatre, it became abundantly clear that we still lacked the elementary tools for any kind of critical operation on Pinter. His action and characters undoubtedly possessed their own inner logic; there was no question of their theatrical impact. But the nature of that logic and impact were still Pinter's secret. To one disgusted woman in the first night audience, however, the secret was wide open. "These people," she said, "they're just like animals."

I don't suppose for a minute that Pinter prepared himself for the theater by a study of ethology; at the time he was writing his first plays the only available nonspecialist work on the subject was Lorenz's *King Solomon's Ring*. It nevertheless remains a fact that most of his plays from *The Room* onward yield themselves as easily to ethological interpretation as they defy psychological and economic analysis. The Pinter character has no politics, no opinions, no affections or speculative intelligence, and no personal psychology. He is there to defend his room. If anyone invades it he is on his defenses; the intruder may be a victim, an ally, or an assailant. Until the proprietor finds out which, there is talk, a verbal tournament to decide who will gain the dominant position and territorial rights. As the lady said, it is like animals talking.

There are outbreaks of violence in Pinter's plays, but they are infrequent and usually displaced from the climactic positions in the action. His stage does not present the conventional image of a jungle. There is much routine hospitality, much apparently aimless chat, and much silence. What is taking place is a vigilant maneuver over ground which is no less ruthless for being conducted without extravagant gestures. Pinter himself had some illuminating points to make about this in a television interview in the summer of 1968. He began by speaking of his time as an actor with Donald Wolfit, the last of Britain's barnstorming actor-managers:

> I was playing one of Lear's knights, and I remember we were all pretty much in the shadows, with Wolfit standing on a very high rostrum with his back to the audience, with his cloak. There was a spotlight on him. And at a certain moment—it was the most tingling experience to be on stage with him and watching this happen every night—the cloak would *fling* right round. It was quite a shattering moment. It's that *taking* of dramatic moments that was unparalleled. One doesn't see anything like that these days, except for Sir Laurence Olivier. And so far as I'm concerned, there are comparable moments in what I seem to write. The moments are very exact and even very small, perhaps even trivial—as when a glass is moved from there to there. Now, in my terms I feel that this is a very big moment, a very important moment. You haven't got the cloak, but you do have the glass.

This view gets a transatlantic echo from John Updike:

> We live in a world . . . where the decisive deed may invite the holocaust. . . . Introversion, perhaps, has been forced upon history; an age of nuance, of ambiguous gestures and psychological jockeying on a national and private scale, is upon us.

It is this age, too, that has brought forth the new biology. With the image of innate human dignity irreparably defaced by the bestial history of the past thirty years, we are only too ready to claim kinship with the animals. The old ideologies of the century have done nothing to arrest human self-destruction. So now we are prepared to learn from Lorenz's geese and Jane Goodall's chimpanzees; to accept territory rather than sex as the mainspring of our behavior; to acknowledge the murder weapon as the first human invention and the main index of subsequent cultural growth; and to view ourselves, unhappily torn between free intelligence and innate behavior patterns, as the missing link.

Whether or not ethology will prove a more reliable aid to human survival than any precious blueprint for mankind is not the point. You cannot live in the modern world without taking it in through the pores and finding new applications of it every day, either in your trouble with the neighbors or in the news from Czechoslovakia and Nigeria (not to mention Vietnam and the Six-Day War).

So far as Pinter is concerned, let's take a handful of passages for which no rational explanation, so far as I know, has been offered. In *The Room*, for instance, a husband returns home to find that the landlord has visited his wife with a pair of prospective new tenants in tow. In reply he delivers a passionate speech about driving his van. In ordinary dramatic terms, there is no continuity; but in terms of animal behavior, he is simply asserting his power as a proprietor by means of a symbolic show of strength, like a baboon beating its chest. Again, in *The Birthday Party*, the intruder, McCann, repeatedly sits down to tear newspapers into strips, a totally unexplained action, which nevertheless makes sense as a displacement activity such as animals adopt by discharging their aggressive energy into inanimate objects.

In these and other earlier pieces, Pinter used the animal metaphor with discretion, encased in a reassuringly human mask. *The Homecoming*, when it first appeared, took one by surprise because it seemed so much coarser and less musical than his previous work. But all Pinter had done was to remove the conventional mask and show the naked animal. The play, as a result, has to be understood in territorial terms or not at all.

The little society that takes shape in the first scenes resembles the type of animal organization which Robert Ardrey calls the "noyau": a central stronghold whose members go out to work off their excess energies on the frontiers, living with their neighbors in a "dear-enemy" relationship. It is a family of predators, and as things stand to begin with, it is clear that a power contest is going on. Max, the old bull, is losing ground to his two sons Lenny and Joey; for the time being, most of their activity is directed outside the family—Lenny's into acquiring other properties as a pimp and Joey's into boxing. In the meantime Max still nominally retains his right as proprietor, even though he is reduced from his former dignity as a hunter (an ex-butcher, he talks about "going all over the country to find meat") to acting as the family cook. (Immediately we are on thin ice. Pinter always destroys things by explicit reference; nobody's word is to be trusted. But as nobody challenges Max's statements about his past, it's fair to take them as more than a mere strategic fantasy.) On the margin is Max's younger brother Sam, the weakling of the pack, a hired-car chauffeur who owns nothing of his own and likes to paw enviously at other people's possessions, such as Max's dead wife. He tries to make himself useful in the kitchen, but Max takes this as a territorial invasion, and his favorite way of displaying his proprietary authority is by threatening to throw Sam—the only member of the family he can be sure of beating—out of the house.

Within these first scenes, two prevailing motives are established, one conservative and the other aggressive. I cannot improve on Ardrey's definition of them. "Through the holding of territory, we defend what social status we have achieved; by challenging our neighbor, we attempt to better ourselves." The territorial side is clear enough; it is manifest in the characters' setting and physical actions. Being static, it rarely furnishes any dramatic impulse. The impetus comes much more from the status contest, each member of the pack trying to enlarge his domain at the expense of those around him. Much of the dia-

logue in *The Homecoming* is devoted to status battles, and
one can instantly recognize it from the quality of the language
which modulates, as it were, into italics. Characters depart
from their normal idiom so as to lay claim to experiences of
which they seem only to have read in newspapers. Lenny has
only to be deciding which horse to back to provoke Max into
claiming a lifetime's experience of the track and long-standing
friendships with the Ascot set. The same thing happens again
and again. Joey's boxing brings out the same emulation. And
when Teddy the philosopher arrives, Lenny, the most predatory
of the group, tries to level with him by asking, "Do you detect
a certain logical incoherence in the central affirmations of Christian theism?" To which Teddy returns the perfect territorial
reply, "That question doesn't fall within my province."

Teddy is a complete outsider; if we have any doubts on that
score, they are dispelled when Lenny tells him he belongs to the
family unit. Any reassurance from that mouth is bound to be
untrue! And his behavior inside the house literally illustrates
the ethological comparison between proprietary and intrusive
behavior. Off his home ground Teddy hardly exists; he is a
wraith compared with the others. There is no reason to doubt
what he says about his life in America, but it comes off his lips
with so little confidence that it sounds like lies. "It's a great life,
at the University . . . you know. . . . We've got a lovely
house . . . we've got all . . . we've got everything we want.
It's a very stimulating environment." On the threshold with
Ruth he delivers a pep talk about the family, telling her not to
be nervous. But Ruth is not in the least nervous. Teddy is talking
for himself and projecting his own fears onto her.

Ruth is the play's pivot (as one might suspect in Pinter from
a character who says so little), and she supports two territorial
assertions, that when a female passes out of a male's stamping
ground, she cancels her bond with him, and that her love goes
to the male who owns the best piece of property.

The play's title refers to her, not to Teddy. It is no homecoming for him; whereas she (even distrusting her probably

untrustworthy statement that she was born nearby) is instantly on home ground. Teddy, however, has a legitimate claim to belonging there, which she has not. And the main action of the piece shows her taking possession of the territory while Teddy is being dispossessed.

Ruth is equally impervious to insult and flattery. She takes in the situation—a houseful of males who have not had a woman living on the premises since the mother died—and moves straight toward her target. The two dominant males, Lenny and Max, both initially respond to her with a show of violence— Lenny by telling the story of the girl he almost murdered; Max by physically assaulting Joey and Sam so as to prove himself, in her eyes, as the king stag. Ruth's response in the first case is to answer Lenny's violence with an aggressive sexual challenge; and in the second, to take Max's brawl in her stride as a fitting tribute to what she has to offer.

By this time Teddy has already been edged out of the combat. His behavior changes from feeble protest to the tactic (discussed in Desmond Morris's *The Naked Ape*) of going limp in the aggressor's arms and even lending what energy he has to the opposing side. The clue to the Teddy–Ruth relationship is in their contrasted imagery of cleanliness and dirt. America for Teddy is a land of swimming pools, early morning sunlight, and quiet sedentary work. In London, he says, there is nowhere to bathe: "It's like a urinal. A filthy urinal!" This is the view of a cerebral creature whose change of country amounts to an amputation of his animal inheritance. For Ruth, America is a desert populated only by insects; it is not an environment that supports animal life. The dirt and aggression of the London house provide the environment she needs. It's summed up in Max's speech: "I've never had a whore under this roof before. Ever since your mother died." It sounds like a joke line; but Ruth would see nothing inappropriate in it and could well take it as a compliment.

From this reading, *The Homecoming* emerges as a very ironic play. Ruth's relations with the family consist of extended bargaining: she has sex to offer, they have territory, and in the end they strike a deal. In conventional terms she seems to get the worse of it; exchanging her status as a well-to-do wife and mother for life as a prostitute with four men to satisfy free of charge in her spare time. But in territorial terms, the position is reversed. The female is the sexual specialist, and the exercise of that function robs her of nothing. Sexually she retains the whip hand—a point which Pinter emphasizes in the last scene when the apparently victorious Max falls on his knees begging for attention from her. She is the queen bee, not the captive. Her own tactics are absolutely clear. She wants to translate sexual power into real estate, and she does so by specifying precisely the property she desires—the number of rooms, services, domestic assistance, wardrobe—and putting the whole thing in contractual terms. What we see, in other words, is a ritualized tournament in which the two instincts of sexual desire and territorial aspiration fight it out under the scrutiny of an emasculated observer on the sidelines. There is no doubt that territory is the winner.

PINTER'S HIDEOUS COMEDY

Margaret Croyden

Harold Pinter's characters in *The Homecoming* are the embodiment of the comic grotesque. Primitive and anarchistic, civilized and sophisticated, their behavior suggests a comedy of primitive ritual on the one hand, and a comedy of manners, on the other. Sometimes the two blend, sometimes they contradict, but most often the latter is a disguise for the former; thereby enabling the characters to move from the rational to the unpredictable, from the mundane to the savage, so that the characters' life styles appear shocking and incomprensible. But what may deem to be reversals of form and order and unconventional attitudes to sex, marriage, and the family can be traced to primitive ritual—dramatized within the framework of the middle-class comedy of manners. This commingling produces perplexing incongruities, but releases a percolating hidden energy which maximizes Pinter's hideous comic sneer, and evokes a demiworld where the elemental and the cultivated interact, where the unimaginable is permissible and the ludicrous possible, where animality is fundamental—despite its comedy of manners disguise.

I

The play appears to be about a "peculiar" lower middle-class English family. Actually, the family is an equivalent of an archetypal collective whose conflicts and desires remain on the

45

unconscious level but who, in order to give expression to their wants, act out ritual. Max, the head of the "tribe," is a primitive figure; he descends from a long line of butchers. Apparently he signifies the loss of spiritual values and the substitution of animal ones, but metaphorically he is the "old king" masking his sterility of age with bellicose rhetoric. Dominating his clansmen (a brother and two sons), he is unaware that this disease—sexual barrenness—is the "plague" that threatens the tribe's power. Divested of virility, unsure of his masculinity, Max does the household chores, cleans, cooks, calls his sons "bitch" and "tit," relishes talk about meat, and recalls with pleasure his slaughter of animals—a sadistic joy that gives him a sense of fecundity and power.

The family's continual reference to animals confirms their primitive world view, and primitive self-image. Lenny, the elder son, accuses his father of "cooking for a lot of dogs"; Joey, the younger, boasts of his seduction of "birds"; Max calls his brother a "maggot," dreams about fillies, and conjures up images of disease and filth as he refers to his wife's "rotten, stinking face," to himself as a "lousy, filthy father," to his sons as "puss-ridden," to Ruth as "pox-ridden," to various others as "dirty, scrubby, and smelly." Like dogs, the family bark at each other, using a colloquial rhythmic language reminiscent of a lost poetry. In the scramble for power, Max is top-dog; Sam, underdog; Joey and Lenny vie for position (the latter by peddling flesh, the former by peddling brawn); the third son, Teddy, returning from America, peddles his own brand of power: philosophy.

The homecoming is a gathering of the clan to settle differences—to solve the problem of ascension, for the "old king" is dying, though no one ever says so—hence Teddy's arrival, or rather his homecoming. Teddy had long relinquished his tribal claims to become educated. But his return with the sensuous Ruth from the "alien lands" implies a hankering to recapture his place. His response (at the end of Act I) to his father's provocation to "cuddle"—a chilling moment—discloses not only

Teddy's drive for dominance but the malevolence of the father-son relationship:

MAX: Teddy, why don't we have a nice cuddle and kiss, eh? Like in the old days? What about a nice cuddle and kiss, eh?
TEDDY: Come on, then.
    Pause.
MAX: You want to kiss your old father? Want a cuddle with your old father?
TEDDY: Come on, then.
    TEDDY *moves a step towards him.*
    Come on.
    Pause.
MAX: You still love your old Dad, eh?
    They face each other.
TEDDY: Come on, Dad. I'm ready for the cuddle.

    MAX *begins to chuckle, gurgling. He turns to the family and addresses them.*

MAX: He still loves his father!

Curtain

Max thinks he has put Teddy to the test; for the moment, the play focuses on Teddy's potential for power. But Act II reverses all this. When the curtain rises, the men (all except Joey) simultaneously light cigars, thereby signaling the beginning of the metaphoric rites of the homecoming, presumably Teddy's. Soon the naturalistic elements of the play fuse with the metaphoric, and a primitive ritual is enacted in a situation both ordinary and grotesque, realistic and symbolic. Traditionally, the fertility or phallic rites of sacrifice, feast, and festival either revitalize the dying old king or replace him with a new one:

. . . the rites may take the guise of an initiation or a testing of the strength of the hero or his fertility, perhaps in the

form of a questioning or catechism after which there comes
to him a discovery or . . . new knowledge. Or else the
sacrifice may be interrupted by an unwelcome intruder
who views the secret rites; he is a profaner of the mysteries,
an alien. This character must be put to flight or else
confounded in a "struggle," that may also occur in the
form of a catechism, to which he does not know the proper
answers. In either case, there is a. debate, a dialectical
contest . . . the action is double, since it is both a
rational debate and a phallic orgy. Logic and passion appear
together in a primal comic formula.*

In this framework, Ruth rather than Teddy is the hero
(heroine) capable of fecundity; surreptitiously she has usurped
Teddy's place; she responds successfully to Lenny's questioning
and enjoys the phallic rites. She instinctively understands.
After the vigorous verbal banter, she dances with Lenny, forni-
cates with Joey, and agrees to copulate with members of the
family and to be their prostitute as well. Hence a major rever-
sal: Ruth, passing the test of strength, dethrones the old king;
as Queen, she orders food and drink; the sacrificial rite is over,
the feast and festival begins.

  Teddy, on the other hand, behaves with customary detachment as he subjects himself to Lenny's "dialectical questioning." He responds elliptically and ambiguously; in effect, he
rejects the ritual and its underlying symbol: he is not vital
enough to take power. Therefore he is the "unwelcome intruder who views the secret rites" and must be put to flight.
(This is particularly true as he watches the orgy.) His academic
background, in this instance, dislodges him and he becomes,
ironically, the "profaner of the mysteries." The celebration of
the biological (sexual)—the ultimate meaning of the ritual—
is opposed to the rational. Therefore Teddy chooses to return
home to his alien land—the American campus—symbol of dead

---

* Wylie Sypher, "The Meaning of Comedy," in *Comedy: Meaning and
Form*, ed. Robert Corrigan Chandler Publishing Co., San Francisco 1965.

rationality; whereas Ruth chooses to return home—to the ancient tribe—symbol of rejuvenated animality.

"Homecoming," "homeleaving," and "home," then, are puns
expressing ironic reversals. It is, in actual fact, Ruth's homecoming, which signals Teddy's "homeleaving," and produces a
new-found "home" for the family. Her homecoming suggests
that tribal activity—the orgy, a metaphor for instinctive sensuality—is not only the foundation of her archetypal nature but
the source of her triumph as well. The play is really about Ruth
and it is her homecoming that is celebrated.

For Ruth is a composite of centuries. She says she is a "model
for the body," that is, not only has she used her body for every
conceivable purpose, but she (and her body) is a paradigm for
the ages. Existentially, she is wife and mother; in the Christian
sense, she is the Biblical Ruth aping her mother-in-law (both
have three sons); in the cosmic sense she is earth-mother,
sister-nurse-mistress—especially whore—the latter, crucial to
masculine fantasy. In the Freudian sense, she fills in, and metaphorically is, the open hole in the wall of the house unrepaired
since the mother's death. Her homecoming awakens Joey's
unresolved Oedipal feelings. First he screams, "she's wide
open," later mistaking her for mother, he is incapable of "going
the whole hog"; she rekindles Sam's hidden sexual desires for
his dead sister-in-law; she arouses Lenny's voyeuristic and violent
sexual fantasies; and she stimulates the old man's moribund
sexuality as he pathetically crawls on his knees for a kiss. In the
end, Ruth is only too aware of her power; she blithely drives a
hard bargain when she claims the spoils. She is, after all, the
modern bitch-goddess, who finds pleasure in the contemporary
materialistic jungle.

II

On another level, but entirely relevant to the whole specter
of *The Homecoming*, is Pinter's emulation and parody of the

parody of

comedy of manners—an excellent modern form in which to cloak his primitives. Contemporary masks, masks of manners, are usually ironic counterpoints to one's integral self. Modern civility—language, discussions, and role playing—may be part of our manners and mores, but actually they are tantamount to rituals—different, of course, but not so far removed from primitive ones. By confronting and reversing the comedy of manners technique, Pinter shows to what extent the modern middle-class family use manners as ritual and as guises for other things. Pinter starts with language. He converts high comedy "aristocratic" prose into low-comedy middle-class rhythms; then he reverses the ambiance: instead of an upper-class drawing room, he depicts a middle-class parlor; and instead of romanticizing the conventional "gay couple," he presents the calculating "shrewd couple." In all cases, he retains the amusing verbal banter as the foundation of the action. Thus, by cleverly manipulating stylistic devices, he seduces the audience with overt comedy only to assault them with covert menace.

When comedy of manners first appeared as a genre, one of its characteristics was the brilliant and scintillating dialogue between equally matched wits. Moreover, such plays expressed the hypocrisy and stratagem of fools and fops, as well as the artifice and absurdity of the upper-classes in general. No ordinary or colloquial language was appropriate for the complexities of depicting a society who valued, above all, outer appearances. Playwrights like Congreve, Farquhar, and Wycherley recognized the difficulty of using language to express affection artfully, and developed, therefore, a baroque and elaborate style, which in itself became a convention. Bons mots, clever antithetical phrasing, perfect parallelisms, *doubles-entendres*, neat retorts were stylistically stylish. What seems today an affectation became acceptable, amusing, and conventional, a skillful device for conveying the artificiality of the times.

Pinter reverses all this. Language in *The Homecoming* is economical and unelaborate. Balanced cadences, bareboned nouns and eurythmic colloquialisms produce a low comedy not of the conventional burlesque or slapstick type, but of the black humor, kitchen-sink variety. The rhythms—monosyllabic and stark—are contrapuntal to surface action and not only add a poetic touch to a menacing situation but release the wit and intrigue of the play. In the comedy of manners, wit and intrigue resulted from the characters' insouciance and charm. Also the double and triple subplots helped; they were fast moving and instrinsically farcical. But Pinter discards linear plots altogether. Plot in *The Homecoming* is a structural metaphor; it is language that Pinter concentrates on, and language is controlled through poetic precision rather than baroque contrivances. In fact, for Pinter, language itself is action; whereas in the comedy of manners language is superimposed upon action.

In *The Homecoming* certain well-placed nouns, repeated words, ambiguous ellipses, and deliberate silences evoke image and feeling despite the plot's stasis. Take the pause. During a silence, the characters regroup their psychic forces, plan their next moves, control or hide their aggressions, ward off expectant blows from opponents, and prepare the audience for the unpredictable; as a result, pauses frequently evoke a wry, black humor. When Lenny and Teddy meet after many years, pauses instantly disclose their past animosity. As each tries to conceal his mutual antagonism, responses become irrelevant, dissociated—even comic. With the first and second pause, the brothers reveal their painful detachment; but the third induces Lenny to reveal, gratuitously, his cat-prowling habits—a comic incongruity in the scene and an exposure of his inner disarray. After still another silence, Teddy tries to communicate once again with Lenny, but the latter, out of context, tells about his "tick"—not only a pun on time, but another expression of his malaise. Pauses are extremely repetitive now, as the brothers desperately try to control their animus. Repeated words like "sleep" and "bed" indicate their hope of escaping confrontation. Finally they try zany, perplexing, redundant banalities because the characters dare not say what they really feel. Unlike the comedy of manners dialogue, the language is circuitous and absurd; it functions as a means of hiding rather than exposing feeling.

In the comedy of manners, politeness, and exacting if not exquisite manners are central to the depiction of the upper-classes. The aristocrats lived in a world of pretension; they behaved like men of honor but in actual fact were rogues and scoundrels. Small but witty talk, shrewd observations, and ruthless adherence to social stratification were their methods of hiding the vulgarity beneath surface appearances. The elite wanted the world to admire their "gentility," their "order," their "good taste"—indeed their general life style. But the playwrights (themselves part of that world) were quick to perceive and satirize the discrepancy between outer manners and inner nature. The result was hilarious comedy.

Far from the urbanities of high living, Pinter stresses the crudities of low living. Without masking its vulgarity, the family in The Homecoming sound off in a drawing room converted into a parlor. The baroque seventeenth- and eighteenth-century furnishings are replaced by old, gray, drab, broken-down, déclassé club chairs, peeling, open-walled ceilings, unclean floors, and dirty slip covers. Gray-dirt clothing and ash-gray faces blend in with the ugliness of the atmosphere. Indeed, the house in The Homecoming may very well have belonged to a seventeenth-century aristocrat; now it is the mortgaged baggage of the lower middle-classes.

And it is middle-class life—its smell, taste, and manners—we see in The Homecoming. Max spits in his son's face; he attempts to beat his younger son; "smells tarts"; wears tattered, seedy clothing. Lenny is equally crude; he calls his father a "daft prat" and a "stupid sod." Even Sam, ostensibly soft-spoken, remembers Max as a "lousy stinking rotten loudmouth. A bastard uncouth sodding runt." The characters need not hide their inner nature behind a mask of sociability or pretend gentility or good manners. Stripped down from drawing-room talk to parlor talk, from scented boudoir escapades to dirty bedroom odors, from chandelier-lit dining halls to kitchen-sink smells and bath-room talk—their manners are primitive, spontaneous, and gro-tesquely comic.

Even their sexual activity is expressed openly—a far cry from the coyness of the comedy of manners. Fornication in *The Homecoming* is not only ritualized but open discussion of it is relished: e.g., the seduction between Joey and Ruth, the description of Ruth in bed, the details of Lenny's and Joey's seduction of the "birds," and Max's continual allusions to "smelly" women. True, the comedy of manners concentrated on sexuality as well, but the social world at that time put limitations on one's private world; fact and value were often confused, hence gross inconsistencies existed between outer appearance and inner emotion. In Pinter's world such discrepancies tend to lessen. The characters actually act out what they feel. Fact and fantasy, desire and action, repression and release, consciousness and unconsciousness do ultimately converge. This is particularly true of Lenny and Ruth, the downgraded "gay couple."

The "gay couple" of Restoration times were emblems of self-awareness and sophistication, of superior intelligence and verbal proficiency. Their charm and graciousness, their essential benevolence and good cheer set them apart from their society and made them the center of attraction. Mirabelle and Milla-mant, Beatrice and Benedict fall in love and overcome their mutual hostility because they are superior individuals—and they know it. But Lenny and Ruth are a parody of the gay couple; they dominate not because of their positive qualities, but their negative ones. Equally matched, they are experts at verbal banter. Unlike Mirabelle and Millamant, they do not reveal mutual affection and the promise of love, but perverse admiration and the promise of power. Notwithstanding, their banter is interesting; underlying their dialogue are opposing ideas synthesized into metaphors and images, into ambiguous evocations and unconscious-conscious perceptions. Dialogue between them becomes a supralanguage in which erotic fantasies merge with ordinary realities and fragmented desires with attempts at wish-fulfillment.

For instance, Lenny and Ruth in their "bargain scene" (one less honorable and surely less explicit than that shaped by Mirabelle and Millamant in *The Way of The World*, but a bargain nonetheless) foreshadow the inevitable contest to be resolved later in the play. Simultaneously, they disclose—through innuendo, nuance, and ambiguity—the content of the supralanguage. When they first meet, Ruth tells Lenny she is Teddy's wife. Pretending not to hear, he asks her advice about his "tick," offers her a glass of water, notices that he's got his pajamas on and she's fully dressed, takes a glass of water himself, is told once again that she is Teddy's wife. Again he avoids that information and talks instead about his desire to see Venice. Then he asks if he may hold her hand, touch, or tickle her. When she asks him why, he tells about his beating up a prostitute whom he "decided" was diseased. Then he acknowledges that Ruth and Teddy are married, compares his "sensitivity" to that of Teddy's, and launches into another violent story, this time about his beating of an old woman. Lenny decides that Ruth's unfinished glass of water should be removed. She decides it shouldn't:

> RUTH: If you take the glass . . . I'll take you.
>   *Pause.*
> LENNY: How about me taking the glass without you taking me?
> RUTH: Why don't I just take you?
>   *Pause.*
> LENNY: You're joking.
>   *Pause.*
>   You're in love, anyway, with another man. You've had a secret liaison with another man. His family didn't even know. Then you come here without a word of warning and start to make trouble.
>   *She picks up the glass and lifts it towards him.*

RUTH: Have a sip. Go on. Have a sip from my glass.
He is still.
Sit on my lap. Take a long cool sip.
She pats her lap. Pause.
She stands, moves to him with the glass.
Put your head back and open your mouth.
LENNY: Take that glass away from me.
RUTH: Lie on the floor. Go on. I'll pour it down your throat.
LENNY: What are you doing, making me some kind of proposal?
She laughs shortly, drains the glass.
RUTH: Oh, I was thirsty.
She smiles at him, puts the glass down, goes into the hall and up the stairs. He follows into the hall and shouts up the stairs.
LENNY: What was that supposed to be? Some kind of proposal?

And some kind of proposal it is. The scene seals an unconfirmed but implicit agreement between the "shrewd couple." Also, it discloses Ruth's strength and Lenny's weakness: she perceives his vulnerability and disarms him; he perceives he cannot "take her" without bargaining.

Lenny is captive of his erotic fantasies which constantly juxtapose the commonplace; his perceptions are out of focus. He knows Ruth is his sister-in-law, but refuses to acknowledge it; his unconscious fantasy life is stronger than reality. Ruth reminds him of his dead mother. She calls him "Leonard" (a name his mother used), might cure his "tick" (read impotence), hold his hand, touch or tickle him (or vise versa). On another level, she is the powerful erotic lover-to-be who might possess him despite his violence, a common shield for impotence. His stories about a diseased prostitute and a motherly old lady reveal not only his sexual syndrome—violence in lieu of virility—but as an act of warning to Ruth. But Ruth remains unafraid; she knows she fits into the picture perfectly.

Taken together, the old lady and the prostitute are a configuration of Lenny's conception of women. When he sees Ruth, he perceives her in these terms, so the stories he tells are appropriate; they foreshadow the bargain that Ruth is to make with the clan, one that corresponds faithfully to Lenny's image. Ruth *does* become a prostitute and the old lady–mother figure —in effect, the object of sexual violence, an agreement that satisfies Lenny and everyone else concerned. The "glass of water" then proves to be a metaphorical underscoring of the bargaining powers of the shrewd couple. Although Lenny twice asks if she is making him a proposal, it is he who does the proposing. His style is to challenge and intimidate, to capitulate and bargain, and later, in terms of the orgy, to ritualize and exploit. In Ruth he has found the perfect object and counterpart.

The victory of the "shrewd couple" (as well as the "gay couple") implies that those who understand the nature of proposals, bargains, and arrangements—endemic to the way of the world— get what they want. To be sure, Ruth and Lenny bargain and get different things than do Mirabelle and Millamant. The latter upheld a moral code despite the corruption of the way of the world, whereas Ruth and Lenny amplify the mores, ethics, and manners of the nonethical, which, in their own context, *is* the way of the world.

Thus Pinter's hideous comedy is an extension of the gentle mockery of his antecedents. Although menacing and grotesque, Pinter's own brand of bizarre lunacy and witty ambiguities strongly upholds the satiric tradition of the comedy of manners. Moreover, in his use of ancient and modern ritual, Pinter transcends the literal and expresses what people unconsciously feel but cannot release: the primitive in their ritual of civility, the animality locked up in their flaccid middle-class bosoms. In that moment of insight, when recognition stuns the spectators, Pinter smirks. "Ecce homo," he might say. And the audience, having seen and heard and experienced, repeat, "Ecce homo." They sense the truth of his hideous comedy and are moved.

PINTER'S GAME OF HAPPY FAMILIES

John Russell Taylor

Of all modern dramatists Harold Pinter is perhaps the most ruthlessly, even self-destructively consistent in his development from one work to the next. So much so that it would be possible, given a collection of his plays in jumbled order, to work out from internal evidence alone the order in which they were written. Themes, ideas, relationships, images are taken up from play to play and thought through to the bitter end. Each answer provides another question, and each question has to have its own answer before Pinter can proceed. Looked at retrospectively, each of his plays has the quality of seeming inevitable, the only logical follow-up to what went before, and yet remaining, until the moment of its emergence, totally unpredictable. In a sense, Pinter, like his characters, is always working at the extreme edge of his being, building out into the void.

If this gives his work a satisfying unity and coherence, it also makes it impossible to cheat, impossible for him to retrace his steps if he comes to a point beyond which there seems to be nothing. For his admirers, therefore, any suggestion that he may be working himself into an impasse cannot but be disturbing; for if the impasse proved to be complete there could be nothing for him but silence. And in the period immediately preceding *The Homecoming* it did seem uncomfortably as though this were a real possibility. The development up to that point was impeccable. Increasingly since *The Caretaker* Pinter had turned to the reality of character, the question of what was mask and face, of whether indeed beneath the innumerable masks a real face existed at all. In *The Caretaker* any desire we may still feel for watertight credentials is not satisfied, but we are never given serious cause to doubt that they exist somewhere. It is not, perhaps, down at Sidcup that we shall learn the truth about Davies; in all probability Davies himself is not too clear about the truth anymore. But that does not alter the fact that he has, and we assume he has, a real name, a real birthplace, a real life history somewhere beneath the lies, evasions, and fantasy.

In *The Collection* a new element enters. The game is played as a game, but beyond the withholding of information about what really happened between Stella and Bill in Leeds lies, for the first time, a real doubt as to whether there is an answer, or whether the various accounts offered may not be simultaneously both true and false. *The Dwarfs* is essentially an extended meditation on this theme: the joint pretense upon which we depend to continue, accepting for the sake of argument that other people are more than the sum of so many reflections, that there is a real, single, coherent entity hidden somewhere in the mirror-maze of personality. *The Lover* separates the reflections to a point where we are hardly at liberty anymore to make our own do-it-yourself rapprochement between them and produce a comfortable synthesis which "joint pretense" will accept as the real thing. In *The Basement* (written immediately after *The Lover* as a film script, but not produced until four years later) even the world about the characters seems to be dissolving, the very location of the action being transformed unpredictably from moment to moment.

Which is all very well, but does place the dramatist in an almost impossible position. For if we all depend upon the joint pretense to continue, he does more than most. Once the possibility of coherent and reasonably consistent characterization is removed, drama as we know it becomes virtually impossible. If the joint pretense is shattered, how can the dramatist hope to shape or make sense of his material? After a pause of some eighteen months, Pinter supplied his own answer to this problem in his television play, *The Tea Party*, which not only withdraws from the extreme position of the preceding plays, but actually vividly dramatizes that withdrawal. In it Disson, an apparently very successful businessman, is in a state of anguish resultant, apparently, on his perceiving with unusual clarity the frailty of the conventions of appearance upon which everyday life is based. Is his wife's brother in fact her lover, or both, or neither? Were they brought up where and how they say they were, or not, or both yes and no? We start with him, and up to a certain point in the play we see things through his eyes. But then we come gradually to appreciate that Disson is in fact going mad. If, in a game of ping-pong, he goes to hit two balls simultaneously, it is not necessarily because two, or an infinite number of balls are or may be coming at him, but simply that, for more or less complex reasons connected with his own mental situation he sees two balls when in fact, "really," there is only one. That is, what we are seeing is not to be taken as an image of the world as it is, but just as one man's increasingly demented view of it.

The two viewpoints fight it out during the climactic tea party, when Disson's view of it and our "objective" view are intercut, until finally the objective wins out and we are left decisively outside the character, in objective reality, looking at him in a state of complete trance, unseeing, unhearing, paralyzed (literally) by his own inability to make sense of the world around him. His situation at the end of the play might almost be symbolic of the dramatist's predicament when he sees so many mutually exclusive possibilities coexistent in any character or situation that he has to stop even trying to fit them into one coherent dramatic pattern. If one feared that this might be Pinter's quandary after *The Basement*, *The Tea Party* provides a conclusive answer to such worries by leaving us (and Pinter) on the outside looking in. The battle between objective and subjective viewpoints has been resolved at last in favor of the objective, and reality is reintegrated, with the unfortunate Disson left as odd man out because he has contracted out of reality and into insanity.

So, with a bit of hindsight, it was to be expected that *The Homecoming* would mark the beginning of a new, objective phase in Pinter's work, and that is just what it does. Compared with what went immediately before, it is a work of dazzling directness and simplicity. It is a play about six people in a room, just as *The Caretaker* was, in Pinter's own words, "about three people in a room." True, it may not be quite as simple as it seems. A number of critics at its first performance, for example, wondered whether when Teddy, the bright boy of the family, allegedly comes home from America with a woman he alleges to be his wife and talks about three children and a good job teaching philosophy at a university he is in fact telling the truth, or whether it is just a convenient fantasy which he may even believe himself. He shows, for example, a general unwillingness to engage in philosophical chit-chat with his fast-talking brother, on the grounds that the question posed is outside his field—a reaction which might be thought suspicious though actually this sort of niggling intellectual demarcation dispute seems to me more suggestive of a real academic than of an impostor. His wife drifts off into reverie whenever she might be embarking on some precise details of her life in America, and there are other points which, if examined in the light of a pre-occupation (induced by early Pinter) with verification and watertight character credentials, might be persuaded to raise a doubt or two. But these are certainly not questions which the play goes out of its way to raise. Indeed, I can see no real hint in the text that we should take what is said on the matter of Teddy's background at anything but its face value. And even if there is a mystery here, it is certainly not the kind to which any neat crossword-puzzle solution can be conclusively provided.

No, the play, like *The Caretaker*, but much more powerfully and consistently, is a drama of character, an emotional power game. The homecoming of Teddy and Ruth intensifies conflicts which already exist in the household and adds one or two new ones. It is a test of strength for Teddy. Having got away from his terrible family and built up his own life, his own family, he comes back to meet his past on its own ground, confident this time of winning on his own terms, and finds that nothing has changed. For all his education, his prosperity, his other, settled life, within the charmed circle of the family he is still unable to act. His civilized irony has no effect on anyone; he is a liberal humanist preparing to sit down in protest when the storm-troopers move in and kick him out of the way or, worse still, regard him as too insignificant to be worth moving.

On one level this is very much a family play, turning for the first time directly to a subject which has seemed for some time to be an underlying preoccupation in Pinter's work. This might, in its own turn, be related to Pinter's Jewishness. Though he has always, very properly, repudiated any idea that he is in any sense writing "Jewish plays," unacknowledged or disguised, it seems reasonable enough that the social and emotional circumstances of his childhood and upbringing should have left some mark. On the most elementary level, it is tempting to wonder whether the great significance, the shapeless terror in his early plays of someone at the door, someone outside, knocking for admittance, here to get you, does not have something to do with being a Jewish child in the Nazi era, a metaphorical cousin of Anne Frank. Similarly, the importance of the family, the tribe, of preserving continuity and hierarchy within the cohesive repeating pattern of family life, does seem to be something foreign to British drama in general, though powerfully felt in, for example, the Wesker trilogy and in *Five Finger Exercise*, both works of the new British drama arising out of a specifically Jewish social and cultural heritage. It is perhaps easier to make sense on a purely realistic level of Mick's obsessive concern with Aston and with holding together what is left of the family in *The Caretaker* if we look at the play in this perspective. And the dominance of the family idea in *The Homecoming* similarly takes on an extra dimension if we bear this in mind —though I cannot go further and see in the actual dialogue, as some critics have claimed, specifically East End Jewish speech patterns. The family in the play is not written or presented as a Jewish family, and it would be weakening the play's force thus to circumscribe its terms of reference. But, equally, nothing comes from nothing and it would be foolish to discount or overlook altogether such a possibly important part in the play's making.

The most prominent element in generalizing the play's effect beyond any specific cultural reference is its handling of the inherent character conflicts as, in certain respects, a progressive exemplification of the battle between intellect and instinct, thought and action. Teddy is the thinker of the family. Max, his ex-butcher father, is a tremendously lively, active, vicious old bastard, consumed with love and hate, but particularly hate. Teddy's older brother, Lenny, is brutal, fast-talking, a coarser, more savage version of Mick in *The Caretaker*, without Mick's saving grace of not seeming to believe more than half of what he says. His younger brother, Joey, is an unsuccessful boxer, all brawn, very little brain, and hardly a vestige of amiability to go with his stupidity. Teddy's Uncle Sam is the only one who might occasionally think before he speaks or acts, but this seems to be the principal reason why he says little and does less—and is disregarded by everyone.

As for Teddy's wife, Ruth, she is the quintessential Pinter woman, one who thinks with her body and manages better that way than most men do with their brains. She was, we gather, a "model" (no doubt in the shadier sense of that comprehensive term) before she married Teddy. She has allowed herself to be made over by him for just so long—very much as a cat will attach itself, or apparently attach itself, to a new owner —but now she is ready without a second thought to do what her body tells her and go back on the game, managed by and in her spare moments supplying the needs of her husband's family, thinking with cool confidence only of what conditions she can impose to make the contract best suit herself.

Around Ruth and her fate the action of the play crystallizes. In many ways, the "homecoming" is much more hers than

Teddy's: she is at once at home in the area, she knows intuitively the rules of the family power game and how to manipulate them, while Teddy, for all his education, has never managed to acquire even the basic survival kit. The action is a straight struggle for power without appeal to any authority outside the wills of those involved. There is no moral framework by which what happens can be judged, morality being invoked hardly at all by anyone, and where it is invoked only according to the speaker's whim of the moment: the dead mother of the family may be referred to as a whore or an angel from one breath to the next, but it is all a manner of speaking and does not presuppose subscription to any hierarchy in which whores are inferior to angels, or indeed noticeably different. In the battle for power, naturally the body wins out over the mind; the weapons of Teddy and Sam are too feeble to wound Max, Lenny, or Joey. But then men, even when ruled entirely by their bodies, by instinct, are no match for women who make no practical distinction between body and mind, but think-act or act-think in one dissoluble process; it is Ruth therefore who must finally dominate Max, Lenny, and Joey, just as they have necessarily dominated Teddy and Sam.

The logic of the struggle is impeccable, the theatrical force of Pinter's dialogue as unarguable as ever. The play is entirely self-defining: an immaculate demonstration of Pinter's own expressed ideal, a play which has nothing to do with the be-causes of drama, but unrolls imperturbably in terms of the simple "and then . . . and then . . . and then . . ." of a children's tale. Of course to do this on a narrative level the play has to be meticulously constructed. And so *The Homecoming* is, not naturally, in the shape of what we usually mean by a "well-made play," with its formal expositions, confrontations, and last-minute revelations, but in a more subtle, elusive manner easier to explain in musical than in architectural terms.

This play, like all Pinter's plays, is, one might say, rhapsodic rather than symphonic, being held together by a series of internal tensions, such as that between two opposing tonalities or two contrasted tempi. In *The Homecoming* the dominant contrast in tonality is between the comic and the horrific, often in the form of alternations between very bland, formal dialogue (the tone of social comedy) and violent disruptive outbursts of Anglo-Saxon crudity. Contrasting tempi are also constantly brought into play—sometimes in the basic distinction between two participants in a duologue, one of whom is markedly quicker in understanding than the other, so that he is usually several paces ahead while the other lags painfully behind, which we get in most Pinter plays, but here with the added complication that the slower witted of the pair is seldom left one down in jockeying for the emotionally more powerful position. These tensions are resolved sometimes in a bout of violence (the fight between Max and Joey) or a conclusive physical action (Sam's death, Max's collapse), to let one key establish an unmistakable ascendancy, usually the horrific over the comic. But the very end of the play shows Pinter at the height of his resourcefulness in reconciling the conflict to leave us dangling on a teasingly unresolved discord.

The musical analogy points also to another element of the drama which effectively removes it from what might seem at a glance to be some sort of naturalistic norm—what, for want of a better word, we might call Pinter's orchestration. Studying the unsupported line of dialogue bit by bit we might well conclude that it is an exact reproduction of everyday speech. And so, bit by bit, it is. But it is "orchestrated" with overtones and reminiscences, with unexpected resonances from what has gone before, so that the result is a tightly knit and intricate texture of which the "naturalistic" words being spoken at any given moment are only the top line, supported by rich and intricate harmonies, or appearing sometimes in counterpoint with another theme from earlier in the play. It is this which gives Pinter's work its unusual weight and density; until we understand the process we are at a loss to account reasonably for the obsessive fascination the most apparently banal exchanges exert in his plays.

Perhaps one small example from *The Homecoming* will suffice: the conversation between Ruth and Lenny when Ruth returns, without introduction, from her midnight walk in the neighborhood. The words seem direct, inconsequential, almost naively casual in their assemblage. And yet underneath there is the clear continuing thread of the sexual antagonism/attraction between the two characters, and each piece of the conversation falls perfectly into place as a move, forward, sideways, or back in the constantly adjusting battle for the upper hand between them. Ruth's cool superiority of tone, Lenny's apparently rambling discursions about the clock (introducing the subject of bed and nighttime disturbance), the woman who made sexual advances to him and nearly got killed for her pains (bringing together the magic combination of sex and violence), and the old lady with the mangle (asserting his unashamed readiness to achieve dominance by brute force). And it is Ruth who, by saying little, makes the conversational pace; she is always in control while Lenny, confidently yet withal rather awkwardly, feels his way. Ruth's final masterstroke—think-acting her way into the one unassailable position—is to call Lenny "Leonard," as his dead mother used to, thereby asserting her dominance on the most immediate level and at the same time setting up resonances which continue to vibrate in the memory all through the play.

Pinter has said that the play came to him all of a piece, with the shattering force of a dark dream and with no more confidence for him that it would mean anything to anyone else than the average dream gives a dreamer foolhardy enough to try and relate his dream experience to someone else. No doubt between this instantaneous conception and the play as we now know it much sheer hard work of writing, pruning, revision, the rich allusive ambiguity which only the writer's instinct can give his work, has survived through every application of the playwright's defining, directing craft. The surface realism is perfect; seemingly Pinter's work has never been formally simpler or more direct. And yet the mystery remains entire.

PINTER'S "FAMILY" AND BLOOD KNOWLEDGE

Steven M. L. Aronson

I

MAX: I remember my father.

What sets *The Homecoming* apart from any other arresting play of the sixties is the bright fact that its dramatic movement is completely contained within the playwright's imagination. Astonishingly, as the play moves from drawing-room comedy to earnest drama amid a kind of doubletalk (controlled, however, at all times by a trained will and imagination), its formal construction is never compromised. After a single intuitive reading, it is evident that *The Homecoming* has, as only the very best dramas have, a half-providential, half-accidental "rightness."

Beneath this, of course, there is a great deal of perfectly hard work. Pinter has set his play in action, spaced movements and silences, suspended layers of lines (exactly right in relation to one another), and formulated a spatial aesthetic that makes even his sweeps and pauses resonant. It is no accident, then, that *The Homecoming* is a play that takes us everywhere by surprise, yet whose surprises are entirely functional. This is the play's final success: the persistence and certitude (one might say the inevitability) of its form, which finds its roots in Pinter's sense of the family as a unit at once amorphous and intractable. It is Pinter's knowledge and expectation of how the family works which gives his play its economy of sculpted shape.

By family I mean the nuclear family: father, mother, and children. In Pinter's North London family the mother is interestingly missing; in fact, she is dead. Max, a seventy-year-old

67

butcher, is a widower living in a big musty house with two of his three children: Lenny, a successful pimp; and Joey, a dim-bulb boxer. Into this set-up walks the third and eldest son, Teddy, an academic in America. He has come home to introduce Ruth, his wife of six years, to the family, and there she will decide to remain as Pinter explores the complexities and difficulties contained within the mythology of that special unit. At the end he goes back to America and can never come home again. It is Ruth who remains; the family is a place where anything can happen and be true.

From the beginning, Pinter establishes the primacy of family values. From Max and Lenny's ordinary, daily conversation:

> MAX: Do you hear what I'm saying? I'm talking to you! Where's the scissors?
> LENNY (*looking up, quietly*): Why don't you shut up, you daft prat?
> MAX *lifts his stick and points it at him.*
> MAX: Don't you talk to me like that. I'm warning you.

the play takes off in earnest, its sinister, relaxing atmosphere having been established. Taking each other by turns over the verbal coals, father and son are allowed by Pinter to come to some kind of peace, but the peace is a degenerate, not a healthy one. Over it hangs the shadow, swift of recognition, of Max's wife, the boy's dead mother:

> MAX: Mind you, she wasn't such a bad woman. Even though it made me sick just to look at her rotten stinking face, she wasn't such a bad bitch.

Lenny tells his father to "Plug it . . . you stupid sod. . . ." In this way Pinter elevates invective to a stardom that is never self-serving, for it is only through invective that father and son can talk at all. Furthermore, Max's only recourse is to rhetoric of this sort, highly effective but at the same time highly stylized in that it is calculated to get a rise and so continue the ritual, justifying his own perverted need for it.

The motives behind this invective are never specified, but somewhere at the heart of them is a bedraggled figure, a sexual relic of false and diminishing potency. Finally, added to the general burden, throbbing between the lines like a bruise, is the question of Lenny's paternity. Here the fundamental mood of the play makes itself felt in a large way, and one asks, what is these characters' notion of their own family? How important is this notion to them? And what, anyway, *is* a family, any family? The dramatic action of *The Homecoming* will provide several clues.

Even Max understands that one of the overall functions of the family for the community is to rear children. He was "one of the best-known faces down at the paddock," or so he brags; he always had an instinctive understanding of animals (an eye for a filly, as it were); he should have been a trainer and was many times offered the job. "But," he says, "I had family obligations, my family needed me at home." This catches a note of homely, quite tolerant irony; if his family did need him at home, it would be for purposes of debasement only. Pinter gives this statement some play; these so-called "family obligations" are at the same time, to Max, hateful and honorific. This is a home, remember, without a mother; in a more than peripheral sense Max has had to be both father and mother to his boys (later we will find him boasting that he actually gave birth to them himself) and he doesn't allow them to forget this. Here he fits perfectly into the structure of the normal family relationship: as the father, he sees his function as insuring provisions for his children. Now this makes additional sense; Max is the last parent of two, reminding the child that the child is not without debt. By indicating to Lenny that he was once dependent on his father entirely, he reminds him that he is still dependent. The parent, then, has served the children and the community by providing for the children. But it all goes further than this and indeed becomes a test of a man's general ability to do *everything*; there isn't a father alive who doesn't want to be known as a "good provider." Max uses this, too—the life of the home: the cooking, cleaning and washing-up which *he* does —as a hold over his boys and his own brother. Every domestic detail of their mutual life is brought up so that it can be put down by one or another of them with a flash of rhetorical energy. For instance the cooking:

> LENNY: You're a dog cook. Honest. You think you're cooking for a lot of dogs ...
> MAX: I said shove off out of it, that's what I said.
> LENNY: You'll go before me, Dad, if you talk to me in that tone of voice.
> MAX: Will I, you bitch?

Here Pinter .has captured the semi-inhibited stridency of a fraught and complicated relationship, the eerie thwartedness of the feelings that pass very often between fathers and sons. He has gotten down exactly its yappy tonal quality. Everything here is "right"; Lenny knows how best to strike home to Max's heart—the careful way he insinuates "Dad" into every verbal exchange he has with his father, as if that weren't the very point. He is so successfully irritating that later Max exclaims, both as warning and prolonged cry, "Stop calling me Dad. Just stop all that calling me Dad, do you understand?"

In the above passage, there is Max's revealing direct reference to Lenny as a "bitch." Now a bitch may be a female dog or a disagreeable woman, but in no case may it correctly refer to a man or anything masculine. Yet here Max has used it with shrewd and satanic accuracy; thick with correct nuance, it threatens very nicely Lenny's slick masculinity. Lenny is more flexible than Max in the games he can play. He reverts to a stand-up night club comic bit, a routine of a strategic child:

> LENNY: Oh, Daddy, you're not going to use your stick on me, are you? Eh? Don't use your stick on me, Daddy.

No, please. It wasn't my fault, it was one of the others.
I haven't done anything wrong, Dad, honest. Don't
clout me with that stick, Dad.

So the games go on—games from which Max and Lenny shrink
momentarily but to which they inevitably return—as shrill and
temperamental and full of chilling verve as before. Sometimes
they seem on the brink of screeching. Living in close proximity
day and night, Max and Lenny have to endure, by definition, all
the additional disruptive irritations of a family unit, so that the
sounds of people brushing their teeth, urinating, or snoring in
their sleep become poisonous and oppressive.

Max, above all, is the oppressor: of Joey, his boxer son, of his
own brother Sam, a mild-mannered chauffeur, but especially of
Lenny. Toward Joey and Sam the nastiness is clear cut enough
to understand and define. But some entirely private perspective
governs what goes on with Lenny:

LENNY: You used to tuck me up in bed every night . . .
MAX: I'll give you a proper tuck up one of these nights,
         son. You mark my word.

They look at each other.

Max is flirting with the boy! And with the whole notion of
family as well. What is the motivation behind this pose? The
father attracting the son? Max clearly has an ambivalent sexual
notion of himself. It is true that the other characters here don't
reflect this directly; they don't call *him* a bitch, or an old lady,
perhaps because this doesn't occur to them or because this
would be absolutely too frightening for him to hear. (They are
already in a situation of quite considerable tension: "I'll give
you a proper tuck up one of these nights, son.") No, Max's
hatred and bitterness are not only purely attitudinal. *If* Lenny
is not his son, then Max has no right to harass him—there
seems to be some unspoken, unanalyzed familial pattern that
the father can harass as long as he maintains his power over the

son. But what happens when the paternity of the son is ambivalent? What, then, is the province of his power? Just how far does he hold sway then? This is the family into the heart of which Ruth and Teddy walk.

II

MAX: You'll drown in your own blood.

Ruth, poised at first, ready but purposeless, smells trouble; there's an enemy in the house. Who? It seems to her that something decisive is imminent and she is startled by the approach of it. Whatever it is she wants to dodge it, to gain time. But Teddy says, "We're bound to stay . . . for a few days." Now Pinter—skilled, discreet—gets the structural machinery going. In brilliant counterpoint Ruth piously invokes her own family to get Teddy away from his. She already senses that something will happen to *her* power, to that familial unit that she, Teddy, and their children constitute. "I think," she says, "the children . . . might be missing us." An equality of concern, for to say that is to call her husband back to his proper and adult role, to call him away while there is still time from being a child in *his* family, from being somebody's son to being somebody's father and provider. Here is a parent offered, in his own children, an excuse which will enable him to avoid the problem of being a child again himself. Lost as he is in reverie, Teddy doesn't take the offer up. "I was born here, do you realize that?" he asks Ruth. "I know," she answers at once, but with an indication of genuine obliquity. For if this house, whose legitimate, self-perpetuating malaise she already recognizes, was the world of Teddy's, of childhood's legendary innocence, then what?

While Teddy is upstairs, Ruth's apprehensiveness locates itself, shifts from the imagination into life itself, and becomes a menace—and a man. Lenny confronts her: "You must be connected with my brother in some way. The one who's been abroad." Ruth replies, "I'm his wife." While Lenny goes into an incantory declaration about being troubled by the tick of a clock, Ruth feels a vague dull feeling, a kind of weakness, a faint but perceptible dread. Lenny again: "What, you sort of live with him over there, do you?" Ruth answers, "We're married." One may well ask what Pinter is doing here. "I'm his wife." "We're married." Ruth is merely trying to establish who she is; Lenny doesn't know. Her husband hasn't provided her with a powerful enough entry line, he hasn't structured it. She is, after all, a guest in Lenny's house! But Lenny will forgive a little confusion in the name of the future of their nice happy family; he is soon confessing to her that he has often wished he was as "sensitive" as his brother, Ted:

RUTH: Have you?
LENNY: Oh yes. Oh yes, very much so . . .

This has a nice chemical quality. If Lenny thinks his brother is sensitive, then he, Lenny, is insensitive. At one swoop, Ruth is denying both of them sensitivity.

The erotically charged scene which follows between Ruth and Lenny both narrows and intensifies the play's perspective. Out of these sexual confrontations will come Pinter's own dramatic definition for the family, a definition which has reinforced the play's very dramatic structure. The words now have the quality of seeming accidental, mere evasions, replacements for physicality. Language will lead to revelation; words will be spoken, exchanged, and an aspect of character, however aberrant, will be spotlit. Pinter is doing a sort of double bookkeeping here: exploiting vocabulary to make it possible to say, at one and the same time, two different, sometimes opposite things. Beneath the lines we can feel the pressure of something big growing, of Ruth preparing herself for her new eventual life in the family and the comfort and security she will find, perversely, in pair after pair of uncaring, though familial, arms. The glass of water that she makes Lenny drink is the realness of her own sexuality, exploited now for the first time, in the presence of a highly anxious male who bears a close relationship to *her* male:

> LENNY: Just give me the glass.
> RUTH: No.
> *Pause.*
> LENNY: I'll take it, then.
> RUTH: If you take the glass . . . I'll take you.
> *Pause.*
> LENNY: How about me taking the glass without you taking me?
> RUTH: Why don't I just take you?

Ruth retires; Max enters. Again the structure of the play shows itself to be impeccable. Lenny and Max talk. Lenny has a question he's been meaning to ask for some time now: "That night . . . you know . . . the night you got me . . . that night with Mum, what was it like? . . . What was the background to it?" What he wants to know are the true facts of that particular night, the night he was made "in the image of those two people *at it*." Max answers, with real helplessness, "You'll drown in your own blood."

Over the gulf that they're facing here this is especially interesting. What, in other words, is blood knowledge? What Lenny is asking is, how *do* you understand blood? Is he asking only what his conception was like? Probably not. What possibly does it have to do with him now? No, a larger question is being asked and whether or not Max is the father doesn't matter now because he behaves as if he were. This more fundamental question, of blood knowledge, is at the center of Pinter's conception of the family.

"You'll drown in your own blood," Max has said.* Lenny

---

* A *Paris Review* interview (*Writers at Work: Paris Review Interviews*, New York: Viking Press, 1967) with Pinter reproduces a manuscript page

replies, "I should have asked my dear mother." Max spits at him.

And now we *can* ask what indeed was that night like. Not only can Max not remember what it was like, perhaps he wasn't even there. After all, how can the same father and mother beget three children so physically dissimilar? Something is rotten in North London. Lenny knows this. So does Max, and spit is the right formal expression of his contempt—for himself, for his inability to answer. He cannot answer; spit is both the answer and a replacement for the answer.

The father theme informs other areas of the play. From the talk Max has with his small, whipped brother, Sam, it is clear that, though he recalls and calls upon their own dead father, if he remembers him at all, it is only very indistinctly. The "dad" Max speaks of as his own could be anybody's—or nobody's. And that's the point again—about family, about blood knowledge. In the fuzzy convolutions that comprise these memories, there is total indifference to personality. Even this crucial, blood-tinged speech is blurred on purpose:

MAX: Well, I'll tell you one thing. I respected my father not only as a man but a number one butcher! And to prove it I followed him into the shop. I learned to carve a carcass at his knee. I commemorated his name in blood. I gave birth to three grown men! All on my own bat.

This is the whole story, the thing itself. Here we catch Max in the process of becoming himself. Max followed his father into the butcher business for the same reason fishermen's sons follow their fathers into fishing: to define their maleness by

---

from *The Homecoming* in which Pinter had written, in his own hand "Drown in your own bastard blood." This must have seemed on second thought too intentional: the "bastard" must be unspoken, never stated, but always a hint of it there. Or, on the other hand, he could see people reading "bastard" as "illegitimate" and he wants to leave that question open, a mere suggestion.

assuming their fathers' roles. And what messages must a father-to-be give off if not those of maleness? This passage constitutes a desperately concentrated symbolic truth—not the truth of fact but the truth of truth, as D. H. Lawrence said. Max gave birth to his children all by himself, or so he has it, and now he will commemorate their names also, in blood. This symbolic dismemberment is accomplished by a demeaning of their daily reality, by a daily working against their own power. Max's sexual self-sufficiency and paradoxically his sexlessness are really an assertion of profound fatherhood.

Now Teddy and Ruth enter in their dressing gowns. In a scene that is at once humorous and hair raising, Max refers to Ruth as a "tart," a "dirty tart," a "smelly scrubber," a "stinking pox-ridden slut" that Teddy has picked up off the streets and brought into Max's house for a night. This of course—and it has its useful fullness in terms of the play's structure—is the rehearsal of the gestures the family will make to her later on. Ruth is "mistaken" by her father-in-law for a whore; but if she had her children with her, the mistake could not have been made; she would then have had a role to play, some authority, authority over them at least. Teddy can't stand by and watch his wife spoken to in such a way: "Stop it! What are you talking about?" he demands of his father, unable to understand when and how things had reached this point. Max continues to insult Ruth. "I've never had a whore under this roof before," he chuckles, stopping to qualify that: "Ever since your mother died." Unstoppable, he calls Ruth "the slopbucket," "the bedpan," "that disease." This is Max's view of women, in fact; by talking about them in this way he can assert his maleness, his claim to a woman's blood-torn "territory" even more than his disregard for their sex. In Ruth's case, Max, without actually knowing it, has spoken a kind of truth. He asks Ruth if she is a mother, then Teddy if they are all his (a subject to which Max pays very careful attention). Wicked, blithe, bitchy, self-congratulatorily funny, he asks Teddy, "Why don't we have a nice cuddle and kiss, eh? Like the old days?" Teddy says to come on, then. Like the old days.

Yet for this family kiss and cuddle they roll up their sleeves in preparation. This encounter might be explosive. Within the formal security of the family relationship that Max insists upon, there is the threat, always, of violent confrontation, the confirmation, lurking somewhere, that a family is anything circumstances prove it to be. Under its awful burden—blood calling for blood—the father and son face each other, full of vigorous contradictory impulses. It is one of Pinter's most successful moments. It is there, the whole story, in all its disruptive nakedness, psychological construct after psychological construct; the impotence of the son who has come all the way across the ocean to affirm the family's existence, "to renew his neurotic affiliations"; the omnipotence of the father still trying to work within the familiar organizational structure of the family but finding, instead, that there is no structure at all. Another difference, too: the distinctions are now all very hazy and the space between father and son is full of danger. A family is capable of mutations, and that is the undertheme in this frenetic movement of associations—guilt, fear, hate, resentment, rejection. Something more interesting than all of them is at work as well —a deeper disorientation that is more potent morally because it is so fearfully imprecise. Father and son face each other on several emotional dimensions: "Come on, Dad. I'm ready for the cuddle." But Max begins to chuckle; the specific momentary alertness has passed and been reabsorbed by the play's atmosphere, and Max turns to his family—the family!—and addresses them triumphantly: "He still loves his father!" But in the context of the play this line is a lie, or destined to become one. Here it is bitter, still wryly comic. But saying it, in whatever bitterness of spirit, affirms that the myth of family has not yet been destroyed. Max is still dominant.

III

RUTH: Rocks? What do you know about rocks?

This idea of the family as a cohesive unit is savaged in Act II, which begins with Ruth placidly complimenting Max on the "very good lunch." Sexual motifs begin to pervade. "I've got the feeling you're a number one cook," Max says. "Am I right, Teddy?" "Yes, she's a very good cook," Teddy chimes in, and we get the feeling that for him this is incidental. The family is all together. "If only your mother was alive," Max says. ". . . Sitting here with her three sons. . . . And a lovely daughter-in-law. . . ." He says in an aside to Ruth, that Jessie "taught those boys everything they know. She taught them all the morality they know. I'm telling you. Every single bit of the moral code they live by—was taught to them by their mother." He was saying before that *he* brought them up! What he may be saying now is that he taught them only evil and nastiness. "The only shame is [the] grandchildren aren't here. . . . " While Max was going "all over the country to find meat," Jessie was at home, "the backbone to this family . . . a woman . . . with a will of iron, a heart of gold and a mind." This is Jessie at last made somewhat palpable for us in terms whose macabre contextual juxtaposition is hilarious; yet Max is so caught up for a moment in his own illusions he may actually believe what he's saying. He goes on:

MAX: Mind you, I was a generous man to her. I never left her short of a few bob. I remember one year I entered into negotiations with a top-class group of butchers with continental connections. I was going into association with them. I remember the night I came home, I kept quiet. First of all I gave Lenny a bath, then Teddy a bath, then Joey a bath. What fun we used to have in the bath, eh, boys? Then I came down-

stairs and I made Jessie put her feet up on a pouffe—
what happened to that pouffe, I haven't seen it for
years—she put her feet up on the pouffe and I said
to her, Jessie, I think our ship is going to come home,
I'm going to treat you to a couple of items, I'm going
to buy you a dress in pale corded blue silk, heavily
encrusted in pearls, and for casual wear, a pair of
pantaloons in lilac flowered taffeta. Then I gave her a
drop of cherry brandy. I remember the boys came
down, in their pyjamas, all their hair shining, their
faces pink, it was before they started shaving, and
they knelt down at our feet, Jessie's and mine. I tell
you, it was like Christmas.

Here Max has found words for a tender, coherent, bookish family dream. The prose fogs over slightly, suddenly seems to open
to poetry (to be used by Pinter to what advantage?). This rhetorical bit of wish fulfillment has Max genial and confiding in
the fullness of a hope that lasted no longer than a moment.
Perhaps here—or in the actual scene of which this is an ideal-
ized transmogrification—the rift in all these strange lives began.
Nothing could be further from the truth of the lives they are
living now. Here are all the shimmering possibilities of a life
they have never lived: a drop of cherry brandy, a pair of pantaloons in lilac flowered taffeta, a dress in pale corded blue silk
—remnants of a sentimental dream that has survived even in
deprivation. This is the informing center of Max's sentimental
life. "I tell you," he concludes and we believe him, "it was like
Christmas." Christmas, of course, allows the myth of the family—family security as an idea—to be re-created.

Ruth punctures the intentional sensuous texture of this reverie with, as always, the telling question: "What happened to
the group of butchers?" Max: "The group? They turned out to
be a bunch of criminals like everyone else." We catch, in the
answer, Max once again in the process of becoming Max. And
he stubs his cigar out.

This dream sequence (there is a similar scene in *The Care-*

taker) has been more than an indulgence and superficial posturing. Cowed, his dream suddenly spotlit and exposed for sham, Max must assert himself as brutishly as possible or else dissolve in the marshmallow bogs of fantasy. Back to his more habitual chest-thumping self, he proclaims to Ruth:

> MAX: I worked as a butcher all my life, using the chopper and the slab, the slab, you know what I mean, the chopper and the slab!

Here he becomes hysterical. Like many other Pinter characters, Max is living on the brink of himself, at a very high pitch. He shares with other Pinter characters a quality of suddenness which can be mean and frightening. He reminds Ruth once again that he had to work:

> MAX: To keep my family in luxury. Two families! My mother was bedridden, my brothers were all invalids. I had to earn the money for the leading psychiatrists. I had to read books! I had to study the disease, so that I could cope with an emergency at every stage. A crippled family, three bastard sons, a slutbitch of a wife—don't talk to me about the pain of childbirth— I suffered the pain, I've still got the pangs—when I give a little cough my back collapses. . . .

To affirm their lives together, he insists that he literally produced them; the arc of his psychological fantasies completed, he stops, breathless before the telling subconscious scenery of his own speech.

Now Max can turn his full attention to the homecoming of his first-born. "Well, how you been keeping, son?" "It's nice to have you with us, son"; "You should have told me you were married." He'd have sent a present. "I'd have given you a white wedding. . . . You're my first-born. I'd have dropped everything." Max relishes the chance to be a patriarch with the first-

born who has gone off and gotten married without telling him
and thus has betrayed the family unit. Later, however, he says:
"I want you both to know that you have my blessing." His tone
and idiom are the fond, silly, traditional embellishments offered
by Any-Dad. Whenever Max is being Dad, he speaks in the same
clichés he uses to conjure his own dream-father. "I want you
both to know that you have my blessing," Max says, relishing
the effect. Suddenly, now that the father has given his familial
blessing to the sanctimony of Ruth and Teddy, the anxiety of
the play becomes fiercely public.

Ruth has now been given some kind of legitimacy—in a word,
a role—and she begins to act it. She becomes alive now to her
own possibilities, to complication, to life as an intensity. To
Max's "You're a charming woman," Ruth, who in her new role
has found words to answer the questions she is asked, replies
"I was . . . I was . . . different . . . when I met Teddy . . .
first." Teddy says, "No, you weren't. You were the same," with
a determination not to understand. Instead, responding to his
father's sentimental blessing, he recites an awful list of her vir-
tues: "She's a great help to me over there. She's a wonderful
wife and mother," Teddy drones on. "She's a very popular
woman. She's got lots of friends. It's a great life, at the University." He gives us many Ruths in a stilted collection of ideo-
graphic moments, of attitudes struck for respectability—in
short, a *tableau vivant*. Perhaps more accurately a *cliché vivant*
in which Ruth herself exists only as an embodiment of something a community would have a respectable attitude toward.
Thus Teddy is denying her existence as an actual person.

But the Ruth in front of him has already changed, she is no
longer the woman he married. They have both come home, in
the conventional sense, but things have changed. Teddy has
what he came home for: a blessing and recognition. Now he
wants to go back to America; he has legitimacy and can return.
He wants to "cut it short." He is menaced, uneasy, and so wants
to go see *his* boys, *his* family. His desire to see his children—

brought into Pinter's proper and unrelenting dramatic focus—is completely greedy and self-seeking: an excuse to get out of a situation he doesn't trust. Ruth, however, is just settling in. In this house without a woman she is in a very powerful position she doesn't quite understand. As the only woman among a lot of males who are uncertain of their masculine identities, she can call the shots. Desperate, but as sensible and modulated as ever, Teddy rushes through an itinerary of their foolish week together in the hope of luring his wife back to her apparent senses. Ruth just looks at him awkwardly as he describes for her a universal summer, "bathing till October," which sounds as if it were the excess baggage of somebody else's imagination. It all comes back to Ruth as it really was. Clumsily and mechanically Teddy recreates Venice, the gone week, his ability to speak Italian. The folklore of the tourist. Cool, already confirmed in a choice she does not yet know she has made, she says, "But if I'd been a nurse in the Italian campaign, I would have been there before—" a line subtly and harmoniously structured to show Ruth's ever-increasing alliance with Lenny against Teddy. After all, it is still all in the family. We can see what Pinter is doing in a larger context.

The hard, insistent drive to sexuality, now given an actual dramatic outlet, is revealed as a drive for power. As Ruth is caught up and under, it becomes clear that sex is just one of the vehicles of dominance, a way station toward complete dominance. These people have no erotic needs at all. "You thought I'd be annoyed," Max says to Teddy, "because you married a woman beneath you." Because, he is saying, you broke up our family. But the definition for family is richer and wider open than Teddy ever thought. "Because you married a woman beneath you." At the moment he speaks, Ruth is beneath Joey; Lenny caressing her hair. "Mind you," Max continues, "she's a lovely girl. A beautiful woman. And a mother too . . . I mean, we're talking about a woman of quality." Meanwhile, Joey and Ruth are rolling off the sofa onto the floor; in terms of the family, her "quality" is being asserted first as a wife, then as a mother, and now, importantly, as a good screw. The definition of family is opening up to absorb Ruth in her new and agreeable role. In fact, quite *another* family is taking shape.

So at last Ruth is part of the decadent power structure. She has turned away from Teddy because he hasn't any vitalism; it has been stolen away from him by his father. Now as Joey clasps her and Lenny moves to stand above them, looking down on them and touching Ruth gently with his foot, her sense of her own life becomes approximate and therefore, as Joey would say, "wide open." Too many fall semesters on the Old Campus amid "the very stimulating great life at the University" and Ruth is ready for anything. She has always been in training for this moment to which she clings, culpable but utterly innocent at heart, to one man after another, all of whom—it is the ugly necessity—will betray her. We know that even if she leaves with Teddy, the tidy little home, along with the idea of family, will no longer be the same but rather the setting for a season of changing, interrupted peace. There are no real hopes to talk about, no need to disagree. They simply had lived together, strangers, climbing the paths of American academe, brisk, professional, obligated, neither one ever excessive nor expressive. Here, underneath Joey, writhing under Lenny's gaze and shoe— here, whatever else it is, is a change in the weather of their dull marriage. Ruth has come home. Her home is now here. There are men, males around her, and however decadent it is she is responding to that. She has sniffed the good life.

No wonder she prefers her new family to life with Teddy. Teddy is a sexless dullard. He is not even terribly academic in terms of America. Or perhaps Pinter, going out of his own culture, got lost, for his evocations of university life are curiously inept. (If Ruth, for instance, *were* a successful academic wife, she would go to chamber music concerts, etc. And if she does, we don't know about it.) It was, in a sense, a brilliant touch to have made Teddy a professor, for the somewhat coercive reason that U.S. college professors, according to Kinsey, have the lowest rate of sexual frequency of any group. Teddy, in his own philosopher's jargon, operates "on things and not in things."

When Ruth gets vertical there is more than minimal affirmation in her new role. She acts imperiously. "I'd like something to eat . . . I'd like a drink. Whisky. In a tumbler. Well, get it." As the play moves along, Ruth is propositioned. She sets forth her own terms: "All aspects of the agreement and conditions of employment would have to be clarified to our mutual satisfaction before we finalized the contract." She doesn't want sex so much as sex power, she is more interested in the power; therefore, the superstructure must be legal, political, fiscal; she doesn't trust these men; she wants the rights of the servants—of the employees—clearly defined. She will serve—is not the classic definition of family one of mutual service?—but she must not be taken advantage of in the way of *droit du seigneur*, where the lord of the estate could deflower at will whomever he chose.

The legal commitment is agreed to. Ruth, a former model for the body, is in business again—this is her homecoming—at last. As Teddy braces himself to leave, Lenny puts the point very well about the intrinsic meaninglessness in any assumptions we may make about a family:

> LENNY: No, listen, Ted, there's no question that we live a less rich life here than you do over there. We live a closer life. We're busy, of course. Joey's busy with his boxing, I'm busy with my occupation, Dad still plays a good game of poker, and he does the cooking as well, well up to his old standard, and Uncle Sam's the best chauffeur in the firm. But nevertheless we do make up a unit, Teddy, and you're an integral part of it. When we all sit round the backyard having a quiet gander at the night sky, there's always an empty chair standing in the circle, which is in fact yours. And so when you at length return to us, we do expect a bit of

grace, a bit of je ne sais quoi, a bit of generosity of mind, a bit of liberality of spirit, to reassure us. We do expect that. But do we get it? Have we got it? Is that what you've given us?
Pause.

TEDDY: Yes.

This speech has brought us round to what the whole play has been getting at: that the family is not in fact a cohesive unit, but if a unit at all, one that admits of reckless possibility. "We make up a unit," Lenny says, but exactly what kind of unit? The answer must be that there is no answer if one is conscientious, because a family is a unit whose potential for regrouping is enormous, whose merest reverberations are incredibly complex.

There will be another member of this unit now, a woman in the house again. Teddy refuses to put anything in the kitty to "keep" Ruth. Max is aghast: "What, you won't even help to support your own wife? I thought he was a son of mine."

With Teddy's financial help or without it, Ruth is staying. Max says, "This would be your home. In the bosom of the family." As Teddy gets up to go, the scene freezes as a typical family parting: "It's been wonderful to see you."—"It's been wonderful to see *you*." Max has a photograph of himself that he wants Teddy to take back for his boys. "They'll be thrilled," Teddy says, taking the picture (ironic in a figurative sense because a picture freezes a moment in time and none of *these* moments is ever whole or solidified). "Eddie," Ruth calls, raising his hopes by calling him a nickname and then putting him down forever with "Don't become a stranger." She is left alone with the family, where anything can happen and be true.

And it begins. Max whimpers for a kiss from Ruth, who continues to touch Joey's head lightly as Lenny stands watching this slow moment which implies many future ones. Pinter's carefully prepared curtain comes slowly down: a still, quiet, slow, very slow curtain, whose slowness reinforces the fact that everything is now going to change, that everyone is now going to regroup in different circumstances and speak in different voices and shift toward goals which they themselves change, in the family.

PLOTTING PINTER'S PROGRESS

Rolf Fjelde

*I had to study the disease, so that I could cope with
an emergency at every stage.*
                                    —MAX, *The Homecoming*

Unlike Pinter's gradually accumulating repertory of one-act
plays, which stand in relative isolation, each more or less complete in itself, a separate foray into the theatrically possible, his
three longer plays to date require their greater amplitude to
explore what now may be seen as stages in a progress. Together,
they could well be described as studies in the course of a disease, one defined by ambivalent efforts to cope with a series
of emergencies, each generating its successor. Thus the larger
plays illuminate one another—*The Homecoming*, for example,
demands some knowledge of both *The Birthday Party* and *The
Caretaker* for anything like an adequate disclosure of its guarded
meanings. If this interdependence makes an approach to any of
the plays seem more formidable, it is reassuring at least to discover that Pinter's own growth as a dramatist provides a reliable
means of access to these enigmatic creations, around which so
much differing interpretation has already sprung up.

Reading Pinter in this way, to be sure, implies a high estimate
of his talent, but one which now appears warranted. It places
him among those authentic poets of the theater whose major
achievements are *durchkomponiert* in terms of all aspects and

levels of the dramatist's art and whose total production shows an organic, evolving unity. Between the rare poets of the theater and the routine play craftsmen of even exceptional competence, there is an absolute difference in kind; between Pinter and his great predecessors, there is merely a difference in degree of attainment. It seems, therefore, quite appropriate to apply to Pinter's longer plays those interpretive principles, pioneered by G. Wilson Knight, which have succeeded so suggestively in opening up the hidden meanings and buried connections in the Shakespearian dramatic canon.

> It will be found that each play . . . expresses a particular and peculiar vision of human existence, and that this vision determines not only the choice of the main plot, but the selection and invention of subsidiary scenes and characters, the matters brought up for discussion within the scenes, and the very fiber of the language in allusion, choice of imagery, metaphor and general cast of thought.*

In the work of a genuine poet of the theater, because of the subtly unifying interplay of his imagination in the process of molding these various structuring elements to his underlying vision, it is entirely possible from a single reiterated image to arrive at the pattern of the whole, in the same way that, from the exhumed jawbone fragment, the paleontologist reconstructs the lost prehistoric man.

One such recurrent image was early noted by Ruby Cohn in an article that considers Pinter's theater only up through *The Caretaker*: ". . . in all the plays," she writes, "the motor van becomes a clear symbol of modern power." ** Certainly for Pinter the ominous motif of the van returns with obsessive regularity, and in general it evokes a presence of brute, inhu-

---

* G. Wilson Knight, as quoted in O. J. Campbell and E. G. Quinn, eds., *The Reader's Encyclopedia of Shakespeare*, Thomas Y. Crowell Co., New York, 1966, p. 380.

** Ruby Cohn, "The World of Harold Pinter," *Tulane Drama Review*, Vol. 6, No. 2 (March, 1962), p. 65.

man, mechanized force. But more revealing than any static equivalence of the van to modern power is the fluidity of the image; it conforms to the distinctive pressures of each play in which it appears and like a drop of quicksilver mirrors the central tensions in miniature. Leaving aside its debut in Pinter's first one-act play, *The Room*, the motor van motif enters at the middle of Act One of *The Birthday Party* (1958): Stanley, advancing threateningly on Meg, tells her, "They're coming today. . . . They're coming in a van. . . . And do you know what they've got in that van? . . . They've got a wheelbarrow in that van." The wheelbarrow, he goes on, will be unloaded and wheeled up the garden path to the front door because they're "looking for someone. . . . A certain person." Meg's breathless terror conveys her surmise that she must be that certain person; but in Act Three her anxious questioning of Petey identifies the van and wheelbarrow with Goldberg's death car and its boot, or trunk, just big enough "for the right amount," in other words, for Stanley's body. In *The Birthday Party*, then, the sinister van functions as an almost surrealistic nightmare image, introjecting an atmosphere of nameless dread in the action.

In *The Caretaker* (1960), the motif retains much of its prominence but has altered in function. The first allusion to a van, early in Act Two, continues its threatening character from the preceding play as a conveyer and disposer of human bodies, but here with a plainly realistic rather than surrealistic reference. Mick uses it to intimidate Davies: "I've got the van outside, I can run you to the police station in five minutes, have you in for trespassing, loitering with intent, daylight robbery, filching, thieving and stinking the place out." The remaining allusions have a more positive tone, evocative of pride of ownership and constructive activity. Aston, shortly thereafter, informs Davies that "Mick is in the building trade. He's got his own van." And Mick later corroborates this revision of the image with his complaint that his brother's inability to make his way in the world is "causing me great anxiety. You see, I'm a working man. I'm a tradesman. I've got my own van." Thus in *The Caretaker*, through its association with Mick, the van becomes an expression of restless energy, a vehicle for building, for moving on and up.

In the two full-scale plays that antedate *The Homecoming*, then, the van motif provides a point of direct entry into their differing but related visions of existence, as a more extensive structural definition of each will indicate. *The Birthday Party* presents life experienced as a shattering nightmare of nameless dread; within the basically naturalistic conventions that Pinter accepts, its main and subsidiary elements are refracted toward realizing that non-naturalistic vision. Two realms of value are brought into juxtaposition by the action: on the one hand, the milieu of stolid normality, a cozy domain of corn flakes, breakfast newspapers, and new shows coming to the Palace; and on the other, the agents of the abstract terror of existence, the intruders Goldberg and McCann. Stanley is the connecting link, the isthmus of tormented awareness between these realms and hence the focal consciousness of the play. As such, it is he to whom the setting is shaped in a way that underscores his situation. The setting is a boarding house wherein he, significantly, is the sole transient guest; the others he regularly sees are settled, rooted in a community. Stanley has no apparent family ties; an indifferent father is mentioned and a wife is intimated at one point, only to be immediately denied. In essence, Stanley is wholly alone, without sustaining work, detached from society; and in this extremity, under a façade of alternately truculent and despairing self-assertion, he is perilously vulnerable.

Stanley's potential instability is heightened, furthermore, by haunting fears and impotent resentments derived from the recent trauma that has driven him into his present limbo: after the success of his first piano concert, he states that he was "carved . . . up," in effect split in pieces, fragmented, for seemingly no other reason than his display of a "unique touch." The artistic triumph of one who insists on preserving his unique individuality will not be tolerated by the mysterious "they" who "were all there that evening." "They" appear to be more than the critics, or the concert management—perhaps the faceless cabal of the establishment that confronts the unknown artist. Like inscrutable Kafkaesque judges, they have sentenced Stanley to be locked out of his next concert, choking off the possibilities of cohering growth in his art.

Devastating as it was, Stanley's exclusion is not sufficient cause for the ensuing "birthday" party that ritualizes the pangs of his second birth. This is occasioned by the enforced recognition that he cannot disaffiliate, cannot retire into a snug, protected, womb-like hideaway presided over by his surrogate parents, Meg and Petey. For Meg treats him not only as Stanny, her little monkey, her boy, but as a potential lover. Lulu, his nominal girlfriend, wants to be taken places and resents his never going out. Particularly through the sexual incursions of the women, Stanley's refuge is rendered precarious, and the crisis of his second birth is precipitated by the discovery that, though he cannot enter society on *his* terms, the option of withdrawal has run out; society, the "organization" represented by Goldberg and McCann, retains the right to have him on *its* terms. At the end, dressed in the correct conformist clothes of the City man, his mind a gutted ruin, Stanley is led to the "van," Goldberg's car, and driven off toward the promise of becoming "rich . . . adjusted . . . a success . . . integrated . . . a magnate." *

It has been suggested that Goldberg and McCann, in their largest symbolic scope, signify the debased Judeo-Christian tradition operating to brainwash the rebel Stanley into submission; much in the dialogue between the two supports this line of interpretation.** It also has been maintained that Pinter, as the first truly existentialist playwright, creates objects, persons,

---

* Bernard Dukore, "The Theater of Harold Pinter," *ibid.*, pp. 51–53. I follow the general line of Dukore's interpretation of the assault on Stanley's mind.
** Cohn, *op. cit.*, p. 63.

and situations whose unexplained *existence* precedes and precludes any conceptual meaning, any governing idea or *essence*.* Pinter has left the door open for both approaches; he has stated flatly, "I don't conceptualize in any way"—yet elsewhere, while denying ever having been conscious of employing symbols, he has added, ". . . however, I would remind you, on this question, that I live in the world like everybody else and am part of history like everybody else." Whatever Goldberg and McCann may represent, Stanley's induced breakdown is unmistakably the crux of the play. *The Birthday Party* thus converges upon a disease, specifically a mental illness, whose causes are only partially disclosed, and the intruders embody the emergency with which Stanley, in his terrorized solitude, cannot cope.

In particular this last identification of the initiation into existence, the second birth, with the onset of a disease adumbrates the subtler, more elusive structure of *The Homecoming.* For to those stabilized by communal roots, Goldberg and McCann are ordinary, quite amiable visitors; only to Stanley, the focal consciousness, are they the intrusive nightmare that shatters his sanity. Their dual aspect is best clarified, it seems to me, in terms of what R. D. Laing, in his remarkable study of the schizoid personality, *The Divided Self,* calls implosion, this being the final precipitation of a state of dread which experiences "the full terror of the world as liable at any moment to crash and obliterate all identity as a gas will rush in and obliterate a vacuum."** The vacuum is the hollowness Stanley feels, denied the resources of his art, and "reality, as such, threatening engulfment or implosion, is the prosecutor." † If one considers the upstairs boardinghouse room where the ultimate death and rebirth of Stanley's identity occurs between Acts Two and Three as an analogue to the inner, secret citadel wherein

---

* Walter Kerr, *Harold Pinter,* Columbia University Press, New York, 1967.
** R. D. Laing, *The Divided Self,* Tavistock Publications, London, 1960, p. 47.
† *Ibid.,* p. 47.

the schizophrenic's threatened "real self" has withdrawn, then Laing's insights are still more pertinent. As the illness advances, he notes, "the place of safety of the self . . . ceases even to have the safety of a solitary cell. Its own enclave becomes a torture chamber. The inner self is persecuted within this chamber by split concretized parts of itself or by its own phantoms which have become uncontrollable." * Goldberg and McCann are thus realistic in that they parrot the reality of society's imploding pressures, while at the same time Goldberg's maxims for playing the game and the sentimental refusal of both to face the consequences of their acts can be seen as projected aspects of the internalized conventional self from which Stanley has become alienated. By declining to subjectify Stanley's persecutors with such expressionistic stage devices as dream lighting, Pinter effectively implies that the inner threat they present is actual and omnipresent in our time, for which the closed van and the interrogators in the night have in fact been a part of history, as prelude to the concentration camp.

If *The Birthday Party* studies the crisis of a mental illness as it occurs in the immediate present virtually before our eyes, *The Caretaker* concentrates, under the changed personae of its cast, on the aftermath—with, however, a still clearly delineated memory of the original trauma. The situation of the play stems directly from a breakdown, once again induced by agents of society but here in a plainly realistic context: it is Aston's charitable simple-mindedness, the result of brain damage from shock treatment in a mental hospital some years before, that leads him to invite the homeless Davies in to share his disheveled quarters. The striking resemblance of Aston's victimization to Stanley's suggests that he, and not the cantankerous, conniving, pitiable Davies, is the focal consciousness of the play, the character whose development we are intended to follow.

Certainly, as earlier with Stanley, the setting here is made to

---

* *Ibid.*, p. 176.

accord with Aston's psychological condition: a room filled with
a haphazard jumble of tools, appliances, goods in storage, con-
noting disconnected rudiments for living, repairing, building.
As the furnishings imply, this is a play about sorting oneself
out—something Davies ineffectually talks about, but Aston
makes some actual slight progress toward through his positive
step of tarring the leaky roof. Unlike the preceding play, there
is no upstairs room here, no womb-like retreat that becomes a
torture chamber; instead, all the rooms "up the landing" are
out of commission—as if in sympathy with the numbed torpor
of Aston's mind. One aspect of the setting is auspicious,
though; unlike Stanley, Aston is not a rootless transient. The
building now belongs in the family, being owned by his
brother, Mick. The focal consciousness is no longer perilously
detached and alone.

Again, repeating a previous pattern, *The Caretaker* brings
two realms of value into juxtaposition, with Aston as their
middle term: on the one hand, Mick, the van-owner, the hard-
driving entrepreneur who spins vivid materialistic daydreams of
the disordered room transformed into a chic palatial penthouse;
and on the other, the intruder Davies, an irreclaimable drifter,
whose way of life is incoherent even to his unfixed identity
(similarly, the earlier intruders Goldberg and McCann, who
succeeded in imposing the logical incoherence of their bullying
vaudeville patter on Stanley's mind, had shifting names and
ambiguous identities). Aston partakes of both worlds. His
quietistic Buddha statue, his inability to write his name anymore, his fumbling efforts to repair the broken electrical connection ally him with Davies' querulous inertia, his misplaced
identity papers, his abortive attempts to recover them at Sidcup; whereas Aston's need to work with his hands and to build
a shed in the back yard relates, as constructive activity, to Mick,
the professional builder. The fundamental action of *The Caretaker* is not, as has sometimes been supposed, Davies' impromptu
campaign to divide the brothers and conquer the house, the
subsequent discovery of his intentions, and the pathos of his

rejection at the end. Rather, it is the reorientation of Aston in
the course of the play from Davies to his brother: the recon-
stitution of the family unit. Just as, in miniature, the van
changes from an instrument of menace to a vehicle of purpose-
ful ambition, so Aston shifts his sights from his intimidation
years ago by the electrodes in the asylum to the present urgency to build—almost his last words are, "If I don't get [that
shed] up now it'll never go up." As implied in another minia-
turization of the essential action, the Act Two pantomime with
Davies' bag: if Aston is to survive, he has to be taught to
toughen his too gentle mind by relinquishing his constant im-
pulsive generosity in the direction of his brother's harder
values.

Some question can be raised about just how unpremeditated
the lesson is that Mick teaches. Does he perhaps manipulate the
whole episode, with Davies unwittingly his chief actor and
Aston the acted-upon, who must learn that simple goodness
may be only a steppingstone to the downtrodden? If Davies is
the nominal caretaker, and Aston is likewise a caretaker in
caring for one still less fortunate than himself, perhaps Mick
represents a third variation on the title by "taking care" of the
entire situation and the emergency it poses. At the opening,
Mick is alone in the cluttered room, studying it in detail, brood-
ing no doubt about the inutility both of it and the mind of its
chief occupant. Voices are heard on the stairs and Mick quietly
slips out moments before Aston and Davies enter. Can it be
that Aston's hospitality was anticipated by Mick, and that right
from the start, his cat-like comings and goings, his rhetorical
baiting of Davies to rouse antagonism, and his extended and
then retracted offer of employment are all tokens of an evolving
plan to conduct Aston closer to his own outlook? Rigged or not,
the transference is effected, signalized by the mornings when
Davies woke to find Aston smiling down upon him, *his* charity,
like a Buddha, passing into the later faint smile exchanged by
the brothers in a tacitly resolved compact to exclude the intruder. If Pinter's phenomenological equation of the subjective

with the objective can be extended here from *The Birthday Party*, the arrival of the two at a common stand might be taken to signify the reintegration of split, yet complementary parts of one self, activated out of that extreme divorce from reality, as imaged in the dilapidated set, that Laing terms "chaotic non-entity." But in this case the expressionistic content is merely implicit; what dominates both substance and style of Pinter's second full-scale work is the harsh but austerely gratifying realism involved in repudiating a paralyzed stage of existence, a stage summed up both in the nonproductive disorder of the environment the caretaker must preserve and, humanly, in the abandoned figure of Davies, the caretaker, himself.

At first glance, the running motif of the van would seem to have evaporated at some time during the seven year interval between *The Homecoming* (1967) and its full-length predecessor. We find Sam, the private chauffeur, preening himself on his Humber Super Snipe, but not one truck, van, or lorry in the text. On closer examination, however, the image proves merely to have receded in time and ebbed in intensity to become one of a series of stages in Sam's personal history of steadily bettered positions: "I was driving a dust cart at the age of nineteen. Then I was in long-distance haulage [i.e., by van]. I had ten years as a taxi-driver and I've had five as a private chauffeur." This speech, and the dialogue and action immediately leading up to it, are so indicative of the pressures shaping the design of the whole play that they need to be stated in greater detail.

Sam's capsule résumé of his own career occurs only moments after his comments on the "big businessmen," the "men of affairs" of the great world, whom he is privileged to chauffeur about in his last, most stylish permutation of the van, the Super Snipe. In particular, we hear of his most recent fare, a "Yankee" he has driven out to London Airport that day:

> SAM: Picked him up at the Savoy at half past twelve, took him to the Caprice for his lunch. After lunch I picked

him up again, took him down to a house in Eaton
Square—he had to pay a visit to a friend there—and
then round about tea-time I took him right the way
out to the Airport.

As a tip for his day's services, Sam has been given a box of
cigars. These are then brought forth, examined, samples are lit
up by Sam and Max and pronounced first-class by the latter. As
they puff away on these dividends of a successful day from a
man himself enjoying more luxurious rewards of worldly success, the point is made several times that Sam is considered
the best chauffeur in the firm. Finally, contributing his own
response to the passenger:

LENNY *stands, goes to the mirror and straightens his tie.*

LENNY: He was probably a colonel, or something, in the
         American Air Force.
SAM: Yes.
LENNY: Probably a navigator, or something like that, in a
         Flying Fortress. Now he's most likely a high executive
         in a worldwide group of aeronautical engineers.
SAM: Yes.
LENNY: Yes, I know the kind of man you're talking about.

Lenny is in process of going out, as he has already an-
nounced, to get himself a proper dinner, but his gesture at the
mirror is more than casual preparation; he feels impelled to
groom himself by this evocation of international affluence and
leisure ramifying out of America, where one of his brothers is
newly established. It is a carryover of this same vision that
motivates Sam's immediately ensuing summary of his own
modest rise in fortunes. The cigars provide an important unifying link in the action; invested in these associations, they will
be smoked by four of the five males of the family at the opening of Act Two. The silent ritual of their lighting, the pale blue
smoke complacently exhaled into the air, and the well-fed look
on the men's faces creates a palpable mood of self-satisfaction,

a brief aura of affluence and leisure in the seedy house that both reductively mimics the life-style reported in Act One and effectively keys the events to follow. In the warmth of this mood, Max, who has not yet made his comment, picks up the theme of business operations on an international scale: "I remember one year I entered into negotiations with a top-class group of butchers with continental connections." The thought modulates into a nostalgic memory, like a sentimental Christmas scene, of the three boys years ago, pink and shining, kneeling at his and Jessie's feet. Then, prodded by a query from Ruth, he admits that the group of butchers "turned out to be a bunch of criminals like everyone else." The cigar he now describes as "lousy," and there follows a quite different memory of the past:

> MAX: My mother was bedridden, my brothers were all invalids. I had to earn the money for the leading psychiatrists. I had to read books! I had to study the disease, so that I could cope with an emergency at every stage. A crippled family, three bastard sons, a slutbitch of a wife—don't talk to me about the pain of childbirth—I suffered the pain, I've still got the pangs. . . .

This last is one of the most puzzling speeches in a play interlaced by baffling turns of phrase and plot. His brothers, Max claims, were all invalids—yet Sam is his brother, and Sam has already described a hard but apparently stable life of work from the age of nineteen on. For whom, then, were the psychiatrists needed? For his other brothers? For his invalid mother? For Jessie? For the boys? The condition was serious enough that Max was driven to read up on it in books, and the exclamation mark stresses what aversions the man of the chopper and the slab had to overcome there. What was the nature of this disease, so critical and so chronic that it posed an emergency at every stage? The words "disease" and "diseased" drift through the play like flotsam from an unknown disaster, receiving only one definite medical specification, as "the pox," syphilis. But for venereal disease, one hardly calls in psychiatrists. The mystery thickens. Finally, after Max's slashing summary of the family, contrasting so radically with his nostalgic vignette just before, we arrive at his odd identification with the pain of childbirth. What relation does this self-pitying *non sequitur* have to the statements just uttered? All these questions, so closely concentrated, might suggest quibbles over minutiae; on the contrary, they are not incidental, but central to the play's rationale of motives. That it has such a rationale has been insisted upon by Pinter himself: "The whole play happens on a quite realistic level from my point of view. . . . The people are harsh and cruel, to be sure. Still they aren't acting arbitrarily but for very deep-seated reasons. . . ." * The depth of those reasons may be sounded with perhaps some accuracy by resolving *The Homecoming* into the same main structural elements found in its predecessors.

The first question that might be raised is, does the play set two realms of value in juxtaposition? From a cursory inspection of the characters, the initial impression is negative. Completing a process already traced in its two earlier stages, all the inhabitants of this play are members of one family; the threatening intruders have diminished from two to one to none. Of those whose roles could most be likened to them, Teddy is the eldest son and, though living abroad, is regarded, according to Lenny, as an integral part of the family unit, the standard and example they try to emulate; Ruth, the one non-blood relation, is soon assimilated as kith and kin. This context of close relationships is so intrinsic to the play's rationale of motives that it receives maximum structural emphasis: Teddy's homecoming is made the climax and conclusion of Act One, just as in a different sense Ruth's homecoming fulfills the same purpose for Act Two. The significance of their homecoming is thus unmistakably the crux of the play.

---

* As quoted in Henry Hewes, "Probing Pinter's Play," *Saturday Review*, April 8, 1967, p. 54.

If such is the case, Teddy and Ruth, like Stanley and Aston previously, can be taken jointly as the focal consciousness of the play, meaning that what they are aware of is at the heart of its particular vision of existence. A moment's reflection then confirms that two juxtaposed realms are in fact bridged by Teddy and Ruth, although one of these is entirely offstage— namely, America and England, or perhaps the New World and the Old, if Max's continental connections are allowed. This juxtaposition governs a number of the matters brought up for discussion within the scenes, most notably the affluent Yankee that we have seen preoccupying Lenny and Sam before any transatlantic visitors materialize.

Again, if Teddy and Ruth comprise the play's focal consciousness, one might expect to find, in accord with precedent, their situation echoed in the setting. The old family house in North London has been partially renovated, with the back wall of the living room replaced by an open arch. Teddy comments on the change in his birthplace to Ruth:

> TEDDY: What do you think of the room? Big, isn't it? It's a big house. I mean, it's a fine room, don't you think? Actually there was a wall, across there . . . with a door. We knocked it down . . . years ago . . . to make an open living area. The structure wasn't affected, you see. My mother was dead.

Teddy's observations call attention to the fact that a traditional, confined environment has been transformed, somewhat violently, into an "open living area," suggesting the old claustrophobic pattern of life partially broken out of, first here and then by Teddy still more extensively in America. This implication is picked up by Lenny, who comments that "we live a closer life . . . here than you do over there" in what he calls "the open spaces." Finally, completing the key elements of the setting, one notices as well through the arch the rather sinister staircase ascending once again to an upstairs room that awaits definition.

If Ruth and Teddy have a similar dramatic function to Stanley and to Aston, one might further ask, extending the structural parallels, whether they also display signs of mental illness, or even breakdown. The text here is opaque, which accords, however, with the unfolding pattern. Since the psychic trauma of the second-birth was central and immediate in the first play, and removed into the past with still some memory of its origins in its successor, perhaps in this third play all recall of the source has been eclipsed and everything is now aftermath, obscure repercussions, ricocheting shock waves, diffused symptoms. Ruth is referred to by Teddy as "not well." And Max accepts her by responding that he's "used to looking after people who are not so well." Did Ruth undergo a breakdown in America? Is that the reason for the trip abroad, as well as for her strange description of America as all rock and sand and insects—a wasteland image radically at odds with Teddy's recollections of a lovely house and a swimming pool? It seems at least a likely surmise. As for Teddy himself, he appears to bear psychic scars left by some long past crisis. Like Aston, he has continued to exist, but as a mind not wholly intact. A schizoid loss of effect characterizes him; and like Stanley he also seems to fear implosion, maintaining his equilibrium only, as he confesses, by turning people into nonthreatening objects. So divergent is Teddy's manner and behavior from the rest of his family that one strongly suspects that if psychiatrists were consulted (or if Max simply believes they were, which phenomenologically is much the same), it is Teddy, before any other candidate, who elicited their concern and who was rebuilt to function not humanly, but as a robotized intelligence operating on things and not in things, an antiseptically specialized mind, the deracinated man of the future identified with the clean sterile land of the future—America.

The pathology of Teddy's detachment finds corroboration

from Laing, who writes of the schizoid individual's strategy for avoiding his anxiety by turning the other person into a thing, and then depersonalizing or objectifying his own feelings toward that thing. By such means, "the depersonalized person can be used, manipulated, acted upon." * In the relationship at the core of the play, this is exactly the defensive tactic Teddy has adopted toward Ruth. Emulating Teddy's example, since to varying degrees they share his pathology, the family then follows suit, converting Ruth into an object, a salable commodity, thereby making contracturally firm that aura of international success they conjured over cigars at the beginning of Act Two.

All very practical and businesslike, but still one wonders why. Why the pervasive pressure to win, on the horses, or to the top in boxing, or as a member of a successful philosophy department, or as the sole progenitor giving birth to three grown men? And in the inevitable consequence (except for Teddy) of not winning, why the constant savage infighting to score compensatory points over each other? What are the members of this family so desperately striving for? Rather, one must ask what they strive so desperately away from. Which is to ask, more specifically, what has kept this all-male pseudohousehold rancorously together for years, holding all women at bay? Or, broadening the inquiry, to ask who it was Stanley sought to kill in attempting to strangle Meg, or who it was signed the legal form that allowed the brain damage done to Aston? The answer in all cases is the same: the mother. The paradoxical presence in *The Homecoming* of the absent mother, Jessie, looms as the root source of the family's destructive instability.

Since Jessie *is* absent, and her exposition is made both meager and ambiguous, we can never know exactly what her character was, except that the contagion spreads—in all but Joey, the only one who neither shares nor needs the ritual cigar —from her dual and unreconcilable roles of good wife and mother and deceiving slutbitch. This we are compelled to

___

* Laing. *op. cit.*, p. 79.

What was Jessie – tell by sons?

gather not from the source herself, but from the chronic results. Teddy, the first-born and thus longest exposed to his mother's influence, can be deemed a burnt-out case. In his desperation, he fled from Jessie, or her insistent memory, to *and* Ruth—and, blind to his own emotions, only chose another Jessie, another ambivalent wife-mother/slutbitch, whom he now despairingly restores to her original milieu. Lenny, the second-born, less deeply affected, is not wholly severed from feeling, but exhibits instead all of a pimp's contempt for women. In the first of the dreamlike reminiscences he tells to Ruth the evening he meets her, Lenny threatens her obliquely with murder, transforming her into a waterfront whore making an indecent proposal "under an arch." In the second of his fantasies he regresses to a disguised version of the real source of his impotence and rage, a nameless old lady whose crippling destructiveness is symbolized by her mangle. She of course is *his* old lady, Jessie. In Joey, the youngest and least disturbed, anger and destructiveness are harmlessly channeled into boxing and demolition work. Of them all, Joey is the one healthy animal, whose approach to Ruth, as she recognizes, is directly natural, if unprincipled. It is with Joey that Ruth alters the character of another running motif: the upstairs room, no longer a torture chamber or a nonfunctioning limbo, but a testing ground for acquiring performance data on a marketable product, a mode of entry into the real world dominated by big businessmen, men of affairs.

story of old lady

Max displays the same distrust of women as, variously, his sons do, but in his case the cause is not to be found in the formative influence of Jessie, the good/bad mother. She may have acted to confirm and intensify an attitude already set within him, but she can hardly have known him early enough to have formed his bitter ambivalence. In view of Teddy's marriage to Ruth, a replica of his mother, and their duplication of a pattern of three sons in the next generation, it is tempting to reconstruct the previous generation, with Sam and Max as two of three brothers, and Max in turn marrying a replica of *his* mother, "not well" in the same respect. Thus the determining matrix extends back through time. (As Goldberg puts it: "Seamus—who came before your father? His father. And who came before him? . . . Who came before your father's father, but your father's father's mother!") Certainly Sam, the only other brother in evidence, suffers from superficially a more benign but actually a more dangerously repressed variant of Max's self-division; Jessie he worshipfully regards as a "charming woman" (the same phrase Max will apply to Ruth), someone it was a rare privilege and delight to escort—all the while knowing, but refusing to acknowledge, that MacGregor, Max's best friend, had had Jessie in the back seat of Sam's cab. That acknowledgment, when it comes, is Sam's ruin; his confession strikes him down by hurling the dissociated parts of his split self into violent conjunction, much as if powerfully charged positive and negative poles had been brought explosively together. Does Max already know what Sam reveals? Quite possibly—or other instances of Jessie's infidelity—but like Sam, with much tougher obstinacy, he refuses to acknowledge it, indulging instead the evasive pendulum swings of his outraged and deformed emotions, so that at one moment his late wife is euphemized into a woman with a heart of gold, and at the next is so vehemently stricken from the record that even her part in bearing the children is blotted out. Far from *non sequitur*, Max's negation of Jessie has to follow his nostalgic self-surrender to her if he is to keep his own equilibrium and not in fact become, as Lenny calls him, "demented."

All Max's habitual strategy is to no avail, however. In the guise of conquest, a triumphant business deal, the dreaded surrender takes place, and the dual victimization of Ruth and Teddy is ironically reversed. Again, the essential action of the play can be phrased in terms of meanings implicit in the title. First and most obviously, Jessie the mother comes home to stay in Ruth, as the closing tableau implies. Max is entirely right: she won't prove adaptable. She has but one and the same nature, as Teddy had to learn: amoral, wide open, overtly

the victim, covertly the aggressor—she will in time undoubtedly "do the dirty" on them. Ruth's unabashed resumption of
her old way of life, secondly, releases Teddy for *his* anticipated
homecoming, not here where the family is foreign to him, but
in America where it is not. Can this fresh start break the
destructive pattern extending back through the generations,
or, in the new all-male household with its three small boys,
will there merely be yet another repetition? The answer
largely depends on how aware Teddy has become. As in *The
Caretaker*, the question again emerges as to whether the entire
episode of Ruth's return is staged to some extent consciously
by her indifferent husband. Jules Feiffer has suggested that "outside the range of manipulation and counter-manipulation
engaged in between Ruth and the family stands the prime
manipulator . . . the seemingly innocent Teddy." * If this is
so, then like Mick, he, the teacher, has a further lesson by
example to pass on to his family, one that qualifies what Aston
had to learn about the necessity of moving on and up: a lesson
in the vanity of all blind attempts to transcend the past.

Paying the inescapable debt to the past is what the play
finally is about. In a more general sense, the homecoming signifies returning to confront certain home truths that work
themselves out in life despite all our strategies to rise above
them—the way, for example, that the family lives on within
the individual. Just as with the house that is gradually re-
claimed from play to play: though the mother is dead and the
renovations are made and success is sought and even attained
at a price, the basic structure does not change, and the motifs
that reveal it must tend to recur. And so the van, which
seemed at first to be absent from the scene, proves only to
have been waiting, in altered form, to strike down the present,
and specifically the one person in that present—its most decent
occupant—who could see the pattern repeating and tried to
forestall it.

---

* Jules Feiffer, "What's Pinter Up To?" *The New York Times*,
February 5, 1967, p. D3.

The vision of existence that underlies the emergency responded to so haplessly by Sam is actually, in substance, not far removed from the vision expressed by Ibsen in *Ghosts* or *Rosmersholm:* present life, for all its surface vehemence of protest, proves unable to outmaneuver the subtle forces of the past and falls victim to them.* The conspicuous difference between the nineteenth- and the twentieth-century presentations of this essentially naturalistic theme lies in the manner of treatment. Both explore the metaphor (or simply the fact, Pinter might insist) of disease or illness as a defining characteristic of modern man precipitated into awareness of his compromised hazardous being-in-the-world, and both portray this condition not through direct social indictment as Brecht might, but obliquely as fine reverberations within individual relationships, particularly those of the family unit. Ibsen's method, however, is etiological; like one of his chief influences, Hegel, he is fascinated by the dialectic of both world and personal history at work beneath the present, and he proceeds, after the example of his personal emblem, the miner, to bring its buried life up to the at least partially clarifying light of day. Pinter's method, on the other hand, is phenomenological: the notation of a relentlessly impinging, scrupulously unevaluated milieu in which there are, as he has put it, "no hard distinctions between what is real and what is unreal, nor between what is true and what is false." Consequently in Pinter's *mise en scène* nearly everything is ambiguously open to speculations which, when pursued, lead through intimations of a firm rationale into deeper uncertainties. This, in turn, is what Teddy and Ruth are most aware of, as the joint focal consciousness of the play. In contrast to his family with their distorting-mirror minds, for Teddy a table is simply a table; and where so much has now become unsure, it is best left as such. Likewise for Ruth, the immediate phenomenon of the moving lips is more sig-

---

* Analogies to Ibsen's preoccupations have already been noted by Kelly Morris, "The Homecoming," *Tulane Drama Review*, Vol. 11, No. 2 (Winter, 1966), p. 186.

nificant than the words that come through them, words that twist and hover like mobiles in the air, distracting attention from her real opportunity, the matriarchal power vacuum.

It would be a mistake to identify Pinter's own outlook too closely with the statements—or any other aspects—of his characters. Words, for instance, as we have seen, are adroitly used throughout the play as much to reveal as to conceal the actual pressures at work. More extensive interpretation would further bear out, it seems to me, that the language alone of *The Homecoming* must yield as a guide to understanding to its total structure—and particularly to those homologous elements of structure found through all the full-length plays. With a playwright of Pinter's originality of conception, one would be rash and presumptuous indeed to predict a future line of growth on the basis of structural parallels in his work so far. Alexander Pope once wryly acknowledged "this long disease, my life," a phrase that Saul Bellow's Herzog, with more New World optimism, amended to "this long convalescence, my life." Perhaps all one can justifiably say is that somewhere between these alternatives the larger life of Pinter's drama unfolds, resourcefully independent of all easy, reductive solutions: an ambiguous progress that continues to arouse our expectant curiosity, our empathy, and our praise.

A WOMAN'S PLACE

Bernard F. Dukore

In Harold Pinter's *The Homecoming*, several male members of a family struggle for power over each other and maneuver to win the favors of the sole woman in their midst. Their tactics, more direct than the behavior we usually encounter in everyday life, seem to be a quintessence of familiar attitudes and actions. What is usually buried, emerges here, distilled, to the surface.

Included in this distillation is a demonstration of the human being in the role of human animal. While *The Homecoming* dramatizes a struggle for power and for sexual mastery in what might be called a "civilized jungle," the adjective "civilized" does not wholly modify the noun's implication of primitive and elemental urges—urges which underlie the characters' behavior. The "natural" state, as opposed to the "civilized" state, is emphasized by references to animals. Max, who used to be a butcher, talks of horses. Lenny tells him that his cooking is fit for dogs. Max remarks that the other men in the house "walk in here every time of day and night like bloody animals." He says of Ruth, who claims there are "lots of insects" in America, where she lives, "She'll make us all animals."

Although Ruth does not literally turn them into animals, her presence in this otherwise all-male household does evoke their animal instincts. For example, her presence evokes violence; shortly after Max sees her the first time, he hits Joey in the stomach with his fist and Sam in the head with his walking stick. Before Ruth's arrival, there is a jockeying for position among the men, a series of tests of strength and, consequently, of power. Her arrival provides a focus; the men try to dominate her and to win her favors. Their struggles for power and for the woman appear to be part of a mating rite. There are, in fact, numerous indications of repetition and reenactment.

Past and present are enmeshed. The title indicates a return to a past condition. The setting shows the past existing in the present: "The back wall, which contained the door, has been removed. A square arch shape remains. Beyond it, the hall." Lenny questions his father about the night he was conceived. By implication, the men's actions are the result of maternal indoctrination, for Max says that Jessie, the boys' mother, "taught these boys everything they know. She taught them all the morality they know. I'm telling you. Every single bit of the moral code they live by—was taught to them by their mother." When Teddy refuses to put any money in the kitty to support Ruth as the family's communal wife, Max reprimands him, "Your mother would drop dead if she heard you take that attitude." Then Lenny envisions Ruth earning money as a prostitute, himself acting as her pimp, and Teddy as an American representative who will procure overseas customers for her: "Teddy, you must know lots of professors, heads of departments, men like that. They pop over here for a week at the Savoy, they need somewhere they can go to have a nice quiet poke." While this may be the morality and way of life that Jessie taught, we do not know whether she was a prostitute. Nevertheless, the passage strikes a familiar chord, Sam's earlier account of his day's activities:

> I took a Yankee out there today . . . to the Airport . . . Picked him up at the Savoy at half past twelve, took him to the Caprice for his lunch. After lunch I picked him up again, took him down to a house in Eaton Square—he had to pay a visit to a friend there—and then round about teatime I took him right the way out to the Airport.

The feeling of repetition is also created by the parallelism of characters. Each member of the young generation has his counterpart in a member of the older generation: Teddy-Max, Ruth-Jessie, Lenny-MacGregor, and Joey-Sam.

Teddy, the oldest son, resembles his father in several aspects. Each has a wife who betrays him. Each has three sons. Each, it is hinted, may not be the father of his wife's children. When Max asks Teddy whether he is the father of his children, there is a pause, but Teddy does not reply. Shortly thereafter, Max refers to his own children as "three bastard sons." Each travels on business, leaving his wife in the house. "I was going all over the country to find meat," says Max; "I was making my way in the world, but I left a woman at home with a will of iron, a heart of gold and a mind." When Teddy departs for the United States, he leaves Ruth in the same house.

The Ruth-Jessie parallel is striking, for Ruth literally takes the other woman's place. Max refers to Jessie as "a slutbitch of a wife" and to Ruth as a tart, a "pox-ridden slut," and a "filthy scrubber off the streets." With ingenious ambiguity, Pinter has Max connect them: "I've never had a whore under this roof before. Ever since your mother died." Max tells Ruth that no woman has been in the house since Jessie died, for "their mother's image was so dear any other woman would have . . . tarnished it. But you . . . Ruth . . . you're not only lovely and beautiful, but you're kin. You're kith. You belong here." At least one of Ruth's actions, if we are to take Sam's word for it, is a repetition of Jessie's; just as Ruth betrays her husband by switching sides and embracing Lenny, so did Jessie betray Max with MacGregor (Sam blurts out before he collapses, "MacGregor had Jessie in the back of my cab as I drove them along"). There is another parallel: Max calls Jessie "the backbone to this family," and at the end of the play Ruth is about to become the family's financial backbone . . . on her back.

Lenny resembles MacGregor chiefly in that he, too, is the object of the woman's defection. Unlike Lenny, MacGregor is not a brother to the cuckold (or in the case of Teddy, potential cuckold, for the sex act is not consummated during the play). However, while MacGregor's family "came all the way from Aberdeen," Sam implies that Max regarded him fraternally: "You wouldn't have trusted any of your other brothers. You wouldn't have trusted Mac, would you? But you trusted me."

Finally there are Joey and Sam. Although the resemblances between them are not as pronounced as those between the other three pairs, there is a slight indication that they parallel each other. An asexual bachelor, Sam firmly denies Max's charge that he has been "banging away at [his] lady customers" in the back seat of his automobile. "I've never done that kind of thing in my car," he maintains, adding, "I leave that to others." If, on the one hand, we believe Lenny's story of the two girls he and Joey picked up, then Joey has "done that kind of thing" on at least one occasion. On the other hand, however, Joey, by his own admission, has not "done that kind of thing" with Ruth, for he spent two hours without having got "all the way." He asserts, moreover, that one can be happy not only without going "the whole hog" but "without going any hog."

As we have seen, Ruth's position will be, like Jessie's, that of a wife who may take her pleasure from time to time with a "brother." However, her position will also be, like Jessie's, that of a mother. While the sexual nature of Ruth's position is evident, its maternal nature may be less apparent. Her function with the men in the household is ambivalent. Her maternal relationship to Joey is made visual in the closing tableau, in which he places his head on her lap. Her motherly role vis à vis Lenny is suggested in their first encounter. When she calls him Leonard, he asks her not to call him by that name since it is the name his mother gave him. Then she suggests that he take a sip from her glass of water. "Sit on my lap. Take a long cool sip. *She pats her lap.*" Going to him, she urges, "Put your head back and open your mouth." And then, "Lie on the floor. Go on. I'll pour it down your throat." The maternal aspect, it must be emphasized, is present not instead of but in addition to the sexual aspect.

To some extent, this maternal relationship undercuts the sexuality. There are, moreover, several indications that the men lack masculinity. In this house without women, the men perform womenly functions. The opening of the play is partly a perverse parody of a family scene: Lenny reads a newspaper while Max inquires about the scissors (an implement associated with women). Max's favorite epithet is "bitch," which he applies to everyone, regardless of sex. Max is the cook; he used to give the boys their baths and tuck them into bed each night. On two occasions, he explicitly identifies himself with the role of a woman: he tells Sam, "I gave birth to three grown men! All on my own bat," and later, "don't talk to me about the pains of childbirth—I suffered the pain, I've still got the pangs." Of the male quintet, Lenny would appear to qualify least as nonmasculine. However the two sex stories that he relates to Ruth culminate not in sexual union but in violence. With the first woman, he says, "I clumped her one," and with the second, "I just gave her a short-arm jab to the belly and jumped on a bus outside." This is in harmony with his suggestion that he pimp for her in Soho and the implication that this is his occupation, for pimps, psychologists tell us, harbor hostility toward women. In addition to the absence of sex with Joey and Sam, Max raises the question of homosexuality when he insults Sam: "You'd bend over for half a dollar on Black-friars Bridge." Teddy's lack of masculinity is implied by his indecision and his inability to control Ruth in the opening scene, as well as in the halting rhythms—moving toward a deterioration and breakdown—of the speech wherein he tries to assert his superiority to the others:

To see, to be able to *see!* I'm the one who can see. That's why I can write my critical works. Might do you good . . . have a look at them . . . see how certain people can view

> . . . things . . . how certain people can maintain . . .
> intellectual equilibrium. Intellectual equilibrium. You're
> just objects. You just . . . move about. I can observe it.
> I can see what you do. It's the same as I do. But you're
> lost in it. You won't get me being . . . I won't be lost in it.

The final words are immediately undermined by the stage
direction: BLACKOUT. Having proclaimed that he will not be lost
in it, he becomes lost to sight as the lights go out. Lenny undercuts Teddy intellectually as well as sexually. While Teddy is a
Doctor of Philosophy who teaches philosophy, it is Lenny who
uses philosophical jargon. As Teddy hedges a philosophical
debate, for example, Lenny questions him with such utter-
ances as, "Do you detect a certain logical incoherence in the
central affirmations of Christian theism?" Like father, like sons;
certainly like the oldest son. When Teddy returns to the
United States, he will, we may infer, assume the role of
mother to the three boys. A link between the generations
is made visually when Max gives Teddy a photo of himself to
show his grandchildren. Nor was Max the first male member
of his family to become a mother to his children. In this, he
resembles his father, who, he recalls, would "bend right over,
then he'd pick me up. I was only that big. Then he'd dandle
me. Give me the bottle. Wipe me clean. Give me a smile. Pat
me on the bum." The pattern of the men's sexual impoverish-
ment and distortion of their sexual role is repeated in each
generation.

Among these men, it seems likely that Ruth will control the
situation rather than be controlled by it. This is suggested
quite early in the play by the turnabouts in her scenes with
Teddy and Lenny. Shortly after she and Teddy enter, he suggests that she go to bed while he take a walk; a few minutes
later, he goes to bed while she takes a walk. In her first encounter with Lenny, he makes a pass at her: "Do you mind if I
hold your hand? . . . Just a touch . . . Just a tickle." Soon,
she makes a pass at him:

RUTH: If you take the glass . . . I'll take you.

    Pause.

LENNY: How about me taking the glass without you taking
    me?

RUTH: Why don't I just take you?

The tableau at the end of the play not only indicates that
she controls the situation, but also that she assumes functions
of both mother and wife. Sam lies inert as Joey's head is on
Ruth's lap; she lightly touches Joey's head as Lenny stands
watching and Max slobbers, crawling toward her on his knees,
begging for a kiss. Max wonders, "I've got a funny idea she'll
do the dirty on us, you want to bet? She'll use us, she'll make
use of us, I can tell you! I can smell it!" Earlier, Max had
boasted that he "was always able to tell a good filly" by looking
into her eyes. If his sense of smell is as good as he says his
sense of sight was, his prediction about this human "filly" may
turn out to be accurate.

Pinter presents a cluster of interwoven images: battles for
power among human animals, mating rites, and a dominant
wife-mother in a den of sexually maladjusted males. The various repetitions and patterns of *The Homecoming* convey a
vividly theatrical image of lust and power, and of lust used for
power. Partly because of the consistent coupling of characters,
with members of different generations in each of the four pairs,
impressions of continuity and permanence are created. The title
itself indicates a return which one may interpret as a return to
an ineluctable condition. As soon as Ruth and Teddy enter, he
remarks that the old key still works, for the lock has not been
changed. After he finds his old room intact, he states explicitly, "Nothing's been changed. Still the same."

On stage and in fiction, the family has been traditionally a
microcosm of the human family; the condition that Pinter
dramatizes tends to expand beyond that of the particular family to that of the human family. As the motherless and wifeless

men once more take a woman into their midst, they cluster round her, jockeying for positions of power, moving into roles that are sexually ambivalent, trying to convince each other and themselves of their mastery—while they are being mastered. The desired object can, because of that desire, turn the desirers themselves into objects, manipulated by her. Although Max's fear ("she'll make use of us") may be prophetic, the resultant state of affairs will not necessarily be undesirable or without its rewards, for the word *ruth*—which, when capitalized, is the woman's name—is probably both literal and ironic. Also both literal and ironic is the suggestion of the Biblical Ruth, whose husband's people become her people, though in quite a different sense from Pinter's Ruth. While the word means compassion or pity, the name of the Moabite woman has come to mean loyalty. Here, too, the connotations are both literal and ironic. Loyal to the traditions of Jessie, Pinter's Ruth betrays her husband. *The Homecoming*'s savage picture of the domestic life of the human animal contains numerous complexities, ambiguities, and resonances.

WHY THE LADY DOES IT

Augusta Walker

Perhaps after *The Homecoming* men will be more careful about taking their wives home to meet their families. If a wife who has been living for six years in a high-minded, forward-striding American university community is taken back to her native locale in London to meet her husband's family for the first time, and within what seems to be less than twenty-four hours after her arrival is persuaded by this household of degenerate men to stay with them, deserting her husband and children, then homecomings are not to be undertaken too lightly. The question that is left to the audience when the curtain goes down is at least a direct and compact one: *Why does she do it?*

Why does this Ruth choose to surrender her most respectable, comfortable, secure, and altogether enviable life in the unsoiled sunny American world of modern college buildings and swimming pools, of faculty wives' clubs and busy social engagements? Why does she abandon the glorious opportunity to raise three healthy, happy sons in this wholesome environment so ideal for development of body and brain—normal boyhood and college education assured—that every natural mother must dream about and should be thankful to be able to offer her children? All this she sacrifices, or rather throws away, for the privilege of living in what is certainly the dreariest looking house on earth, in the most depressing surroundings, and of serving the sordid needs, both sexual and domestic, of four miserable, benighted, bickering, poverty-ridden men? Not only that, but to earn her living on the side as a common prostitute.

117

What is the matter with this woman? How can any properly-oriented audience sympathize with such an unnatural, down-right perverted heroine?

Since this is a serious play, the question deserves answering. Let us submit that she does it because she finds herself re-turned to a world that profoundly needs her and that has a strangle grip on her heart.

In his way her husband needs her too. He needs her to help him with his lectures, to raise his children, to organize their social program, to be a "popular woman" and a "wonderful wife," as he says. He needs her for sex as well. And evidently she is first-rate at all those things. She cuts a very smooth fig-ure. She can carry off that kind of routine with flair. She has elegance, poise, beauty, and a commanding coolness that could meet any situation head on. If this were all, she would in fact be the perfect wife for him.

But it isn't all. None of that touches her real life anywhere. And at the beginning she is reluctant to have her real life touched, for she has forgotten it in the hard glare of American sunlight. When the two of them first enter the house and look around at the barren gloomy emptiness of this so-called "home," she is dismayed. It makes her feel cold, forlorn, and above all fearful. She doesn't want to stay here. She would like to leave without even meeting any of the occupants. The air of the place stirs some vague recollection of forgotten days. It is the air that she was born to and grew up in, and all her old feelings, her real feelings, are rooted here. And then her warning fear is justified, for she is caught. The tips of all her senses take in everything and recognize everything, and those deep-reaching feelings carry her back into a long closed up region of her experience. From there on, a few hours is enough to bring to the surface with painful rupturing all the buried world inside her. These four solitary men in their bleak forced companionship, grubbing for livelihood within all the tight material limitations of their scope; their blatant, dreary brag-ging and their hopeless attempts to relate with each other and

keep a household going; above all, the look and touch and smell
of sadness, which the playwright obscures under the absurdity
of their talk—for Ruth, this is close to the world's crying heart.
It pulls at her powerfully and drags her under. She cannot close
her sense or her body to their need.

Still, hers is not an act of charity. Their need is her need too.
Compared to this, her bright prophylactic life among the faculty wives and swimming pools of America is pure surface glid-
ing. It is like ice skating or surfboard riding in keen air
compared to this sinking into the lurid and befouled waters of
the Old World's failure. Those three nice little boys whom she
deserts—they are American boys, and they will be happy with
their well-made sports equipment. Whether she stayed with
them or not, they would grow up to be strangers to her, need-
ing speedboats and football fields and mass education. All
their wants can be satisfied by outward things. They won't need
compassion. She will be gone from their minds before next
year's bicycles have appeared around the Christmas tree. Some
American stepmother will understand this better.

Ruth's real mother-being is broken into by these shoddy and
deprived types who have no future. True giving cannot be painless. It has to drag one through some sorrow, some failure, some
humiliation. There is always the yearning that cannot be met,
but every real contact one makes is an effort to expose that
yearning to the mercy of some other creature. What, after all,
was going on upstairs during the much-discussed two hours
that Ruth spent with the pathetic boxer? Not streamlined sex
—that much is made clear. Perhaps he was just cuddled,
walrus-like, in her arms, being mothered and babied, a treatment
which he obviously has much more need of. The relationship
they established comes out plainly at the end when he droops
his head on her knees and she strokes him in the tender way
that one strokes an old family dog.

As for the old man, who is certainly "sexless," as one of his
sons reminds him, his great need is to be assured that he is *not*
an old man. This is what he blurts out to her desperately at the

end, and for her confirmation he roars beseechingly as the curtain goes down: "Kiss me."

Her real function here will be a pretty ordinary womanly one. What they need above all things is a woman in the house, someone to comfort them and tell them that their crudely-cooked dinner was lovely, to cook them a dinner that really is lovely, to put a few feminine touches into their barn of a home and contribute a little warmth to their joyless ensemble.

Still, all that is only half of it. Ruth is a complex girl, and she has a strenuous urge to realize herself through different roles. There is also a rapacity in her that answers a potent call, like a wary back-alley cat when its time comes around. It answers some dare and challenge implicit in the crooked streets of an old civilization which knows so much more about itself than a new one can, which knows its depravities as well as its pathos. She belongs to this side too, and it takes her like a violent hunger. Her husband knows that much about her, and he also understands that it is this atmosphere stirring old associations that brings it on. He knows that if he can get her away from here and back to the good *clean* way once more, she will be all right. This whole homecoming was a mistake. He had not foreseen how it would take possession of her. Now he is forced to sit and watch, and being a philosopher and a passionless man, he is able to do so, although with great regret. He is the mentally detached type who must stay on top of the world's mess in order to survive. He cannot bear to be in it. For her, survival is to risk and fight against drowning. Involvement is a craving of her nature and the only means to slake the great thirst. The conflict, the bold stroke, the devious venture, are all part of it. The old man warns, "She'll use us!" And why not? That, too, is in the game. She loves to drive a hard bargain, matching wits and holding her own with a tough, crass species, and then to find the aching core inside it. Perhaps this is the best of her gifts. Admittedly, nice girls aren't like that. Or at least if they are, they haven't found it out.

Nothing meets this fierce demand in her good-wife-and-mother existence. Where life is very nice, it tends to go along in a middling way. Where the human miseries are lacking, so are the human passions. Nobility and depravity are the extremes that are not called for. Comfort can always be had, pain is usually avoidable. Everybody gets ahead and earns his security and the respect of his neighbors. And most of the adherents of such a life find all this highly satisfactory.

But for the person who learned early that there is a whole range of experience beyond that, whose heart once and for all accepted the somber and the unknown, there simply is not enough living to do in that safe world. There is not enough to employ human emotions. To be brief, *anything* is better than the painless life.

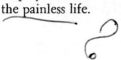

PINTER'S LANGUAGE

John Lahr

I

Harold Pinter has made an event out of stage language. His plays are a display of innuendo and invective, wit and weight unusual in our age of noisy but diminishing linguistic possibilities. His vocabulary is the vehicle of a creator intimately engaged in the lives of his characters and the tactile dynamics of the moment, not just the passive bearer of philosophy or moral forecast. His sense of language deploys an actor's intuition for compelling sound, and a poet's precision, discovering a resonance of meaning in the orchestration of silence, pitch, and syntax.

Pinter's major verbal innovation has been in finding a theatrical form which allows the spoken word to coexist with silence —from which it first emerged. In *The Homecoming* volcanic statement (Max's caterwauling) and naturalistic explanation (Sam's confession about Jessie) are etched in silence. If death gives life its meaning and urgency, silence infuses the word with ambiguity and a heightened concreteness. Silence keeps definitions open, unresolved; at the same time, it draws attention and concentration to the words finally articulated. The abyss between Ruth and Teddy is as deep as the murky silence which frames their words:

RUTH: Can I sit down?
TEDDY: Of course.

RUTH: I'm tired.
    Pause.
TEDDY: Then sit down.

Repetition of tone (even of syntax) underscores the aridity of their relationship. But the silence which surrounds it plumbs even deeper. As Norman O. Brown has written: "To reconnect consciousness with the unconscious, to make consciousness symbolical, is to reconnect words with silence; to let silence in. If consciousness is all words and no silence, the unconscious remains unconscious." * The strength of Pinter's language is that it externalizes the mystery of personality and holds the life on stage open to unexpected associations. The theatrical involvement of the audience brings an insight new to Western traditions, not used to living with silence. Through silence, the stage has a density of possibilities: at once real and unreal, and neither real nor unreal. The brief pause (three dots), the full pause, and the silence are the rhythms with which Pinter scores his plays and which feed this vision, dangling language and situation into complex and elusive interaction. Although as early as 1962 Pinter was acknowledging the relevance of silence, *The Homecoming* was a major breakthrough in Pinter's use of silence, and thus in his verbal power in general. Since 1968, two short plays, *Landscape* and *Silence* have extended this exploration:

> There are two silences. One when no word is spoken. The other when perhaps a torrent of language is employed. This speech is speaking a language locked beneath it. That is its continual reference. The speech we hear is an indication of that we don't hear. It is a necessary avoidance, a violent, sly, anguished or mocking smokescreen which keeps the other in his place. When true silence falls we are still left with an echo but are nearer nakedness. One way of looking at speech is to say it is a constant stratagem to cover nakedness.**

---

* Norman O. Brown, *Love's Body*, Vintage Books, New York, 1969, p. 258.
** Ronald Hayman, *Harold Pinter*, Heinemann, London, 1968, p. 79.

The Homecoming dramatizes Pinter's thesis, the entire family speak with language turned into a game of survival, where invective takes the place of confrontation. The story on stage is deeper than the words which explain it, the language mere sign posts for an immense and inaudible despair. Max's sudden flailing out at Joey; Lenny's fanciful tales; Ruth's recollection of being "a model for the body" have a life beyond explanation.

Silence makes the audience (and the characters) wait for the words. This not only stresses the potency of the word, but dramatically illustrates its inability to isolate anything but the present moment. Pinter uses this device as a way of pointing key bits of information. Max's recollections of MacGregor and Jessie are riddled with contradictions which take the audience by surprise because each seems secure in statement, only to be reversed in silence:

> MAX: He was very fond of your mother, Mac was. Very
> fond. He always had a good word for her.
> *Pause.*
> Mind you, she wasn't such a bad woman. Even though
> it made me sick just to look at her rotten stinking
> face, she wasn't such a bad bitch. . . .

The characters are conscious of silence. If the emptiness allows the audience to hear nuances of insinuation in dialogue, the characters also understand that in this studied quiet, the simplest tonal shift can have its weight. In the beginning of the play, Max and his brother, Sam, have a curious exchange:

> SAM: I don't mess up my car! Or my . . . my boss's car!
> Like other people.
> MAX: Other people? What other people?

Sam has devilishly fended off Max's invective with his pause. He stops briefly after "my." He says "boss," but the word dangling treacherously on his tongue is something else. Could it be "brother"? He later discloses this fact; and Max, even at this stage, scents the threat and pursues it with a vengeance:

> MAX: Other people? What other people?
> *Pause.*
> What other people?
> *Pause.*
> SAM: Other people.
> *Pause.*

Ruth knows how to use silence to captivate and confound. When she gives her lecture on perception to the family, she seduces them by filtering statement with silence and letting their imaginations conjure the unconscious as well as the unknown:

> RUTH: I . . . move my leg. That's all it is. But I wear . . .
> underwear . . . which moves with me . . . it . . .
> captures your attention. Perhaps you misinterpret. The
> action is simple. It's a leg . . . moving. My lips move.
> Why don't you restrict . . . your observations to that?

Cagey but coy, Ruth uses silence with more cauterizing power as she gains confidence. Even the simplest familiarity—like Teddy's nickname—has a devastating, demonic accuracy, when she employs it. As he is about to leave the house, his wife firmly established in her new home, she raises his hopes; pauses, then dismisses him with crushing irony:

> RUTH: Eddie.
> TEDDY *turns.*
> *Pause.*
> Don't become a stranger.

Words are galvanized in Pinter's imagination to bone-hard significance. Their suprarealism, which the vaunting rhetoric of the characters allows, underscores the irony of being both vivid and not necessarily true. Pinter aspires to sensuous ambiguity in language: "One of my main concerns is to get things down and down and down. . . . Always paring away. . . . People don't realize that the English language is extremely exciting; it means so much, so many different things at the same time." * The word is a vivid symbol for ideas, communicating directly and variously. "In a symbol there is concealment and revelation; hence, therefore, by silence and speech acting together, comes a double significance." ** After Ruth has been sexually initiated into the new tribe, rolling on the floor with Joey, while Lenny, the older brother, stands above observing the rite, she gets up. In a new deliciously authoritative tone, she demands a drink:

RUTH: What's this glass? I can't drink out of this. Haven't
        you got a tumbler?
LENNY: Yes.

Ruth herself has taken a "tumble" and Lenny suspects she might do it for profit. There is a hothouse atmosphere as the characters probe the conviction of her sensuality. Pinter creates precise calculated ambiguities:

LENNY: On the rocks? Or as it comes?
RUTH: Rocks? What do you know about rocks?
LENNY: We've got rocks. But they're frozen stiff in the
        fridge.

Literally, these lines are dramatically apt; but, in this context, the words have a larger destiny. "Rocks" recalls Ruth's bleak, hardly articulate vision of America' at the beginning of Act Two: "It's all rock. And sand. It stretches . . . so far. . . ." Her sharp reply to Lenny is at once a challenge and a mirror of her sadness. If it reflects her private grief, it also implies her new control and freedom. "Rocks"—the colloquial term for gonads—also fits into the play's sexual geography. The family's rocks are frozen maintains Lenny. Max, Lenny, and Sam are

---

* An interview with John Kershaw (ITV, 1964).
** Brown, *op cit.*, p. 257.

sexually ambivalent. Joey's love has its maternal tinge (significantly, he doesn't go the "whole hog" with Ruth). Pinter never allows the sexual thread to drop. When Lenny offers Teddy a drink in this same moment, he repeats the verb used to Ruth, now heavy with accumulated associations: "Soda, Ted? Or as it comes?" Teddy is no sexual athlete; his frigidity is part of Ruth's despair. The verb "comes" is a haunting indictment of Teddy's prowess.

Verbal ambiguity becomes a large part of the game the characters play on one another in *The Homecoming*. Pinter creates a stage environment where his characters practice ambiguity and listen for it. Teddy suggests that he and Ruth return to America where it is cleaner and they can swim until October. Lenny tests Ruth's intentions, only to be surprised by her direct reply:

> LENNY: Well, the evenings are drawing in.
> RUTH: Yes, it's getting dark.
>   *Pause.*
> LENNY: Winter'll soon be upon us. Time to renew one's wardrobe.
>   *Pause.*
> RUTH: That's a good thing to do.
> LENNY: What?

Ruth knows where Lenny's angling; Lenny can't believe his ears. If she will shed last year's apparel, what of last year's relationships? Ruth can be persuaded to stay. Pinter's plays do not reiterate stale existential truths about the "impossibility of communication" but show how people misuse what is clearly understood. When Max jousts with Lenny, his son makes passing remarks about his father's culinary expertise:

> *Pause.*
> LENNY: Why don't you buy a dog? You're a dog cook. Honest. You think you're cooking for a lot of dogs.
> MAX: If you don't like it get out.

LENNY: I am going out. I'm going to buy myself a proper
     dinner.
MAX: Well, get out! What are you waiting for?
     LENNY *looks at him.*
LENNY: What did you say?
MAX: I said shove off out of it, that's what I said.
LENNY: You'll go before me, Dad, if you talk to me in that
     tone of voice.

Lenny cannot but hear Max when he screams at him to get out.
Yet, cunningly, Lenny asks him to repeat the command for
clarification, only to use Max's violent rhetoric against him,
reminding the old man of the one fact which petrifies him
—death.

II

Pinter's language is expanded by its rhythms. Character is
revealed as much by rhythm as by statement. Pinter told me in
1967:

> I'm very conscious of rhythm. It's got to happen "snap,
> snap,"—just like that or it's wrong. I'm also interested in
> pitch. . . . I remember when we did *The Collection* Off-
> Broadway, there was an American actor who was in big
> trouble with his part. I told him instead of trying to find
> reasons for his characterization, "Why don't you read
> the part and pay attention to the stress of the words?"
> He did it and he was fine. The point is, the stresses tell
> you where the meaning is. Saying it up or down can
> change the whole meaning. It has to be just right.

In *The Homecoming* rhetorical language is so vivid and funny
that the poetry of the experience takes us by surprise. The
tempo of the play begins with a question and then a strong
counter tone. ("What have you done with the scissors? *Pause.*
I said I'm looking for the scissors.") The play ends with pre-

cisely the same coda, the same moral/emotional wavelength: "Do you hear me? *He raises his face toward her.* Kiss me." The rhythm is both a question and a demand, a statement of force and a modification of it. The tone yearns to elicit a response, any response which will acknowledge Max's power, his force, his sexuality. Because Pinter's plays have an integration of tone and gesture, the musical metaphor is apt to describe their verbal effects. Pinter's plays aspire to a musical, almost ritualistic exploration of the poetic possibilities of language defined most concisely in Susanne Langer's *Philosophy in a New Key*:

> Though the material of poetry is verbal, its import is not the literal assertion made in the words, but *the way the assertion is made*, this involves the sound, the tempo, the aura of associations of the words, the long and short sequences of ideas, the wealth or poverty of transient imagery that contains them, the sudden arrest of fantasy by pure fact, or of familiar fact by sudden fantasy, the suspense of literal meaning by *sustained ambiguity* [my italics] resolved in a long-awaited key word, and the unifying, all embracing artifice of rhythm. . . .*

All these elements are exploited in Pinter's rhetoric which sweeps the stage with the sound of fact and impossible certainty, while hiding other motivations in its rhythm. The rhetoric within *The Homecoming* turns the fire and orotundity usually associated with tragic *sound*, to inconsequential ends. The result is comic. The moral question debated in the play is not Man against the Universe, but perversely, Man versus cheeseroll. One piece of property (Ruth) is placed on the same moral plateau as Lenny's well-made sandwich:

TEDDY: But I took it deliberately, Lenny.
LENNY: You mean you didn't stumble on it by mistake?

---

* Donald Davie, *Articulate Energy*, Routledge and Kegan Paul, London, p. 18, quoting from Susanne Langer's *Philosophy in a New Key*.

In this "tragic" confrontation, Pinter leaves no doubt that there was "free will," a fact with which Lenny toys:

> LENNY: Barefaced audacity. . . . Well, Ted, I would say
>   this is something approaching the naked truth, isn't it?
>   It's a real cards on the table stunt. I mean, we're in
>   the land of no holds barred now . . .

When confronting Ruth earlier in the play, Lenny's barrage of language delights in the sound of its own power, its sexual strength. Each verbose fantasy is punctured by Ruth's declarative sentences—aberration pitted against cool analysis. It is the precision of Lenny's words, their ability to create a strong visual image that momentarily convinces us. Like so much of Max's speech, Lenny's rhetoric has the *sound* of concreteness, but dissipates into hollow categories only *after* we have experienced it:

> LENNY: . . . I was standing alone under an arch, watching
>   all the men jibbing the boom, out in the harbour, and
>   playing about with the yardarm, when a certain lady
>   came up to me and made me a certain proposal . . .

Stage naturalism has accustomed its audience to truth clearly stated. Pinter's rhetoric swells with such seductive power that the audience (like the characters) have to choose whether it is fact or fiction. Lenny tells his tale. As the fantasy spins out of control, Pinter ends it with delightful irony. Not only is the story bogus, the violence outrageous, but Lenny's last phrase even tries to be modest about his imagined brutality:

> LENNY: So I just gave her another belt in the nose and a
>   couple of turns of the boot and *sort of* left it at that.
>   [My italics.]

The joke is built around the certainty of the rhythm's impetus and its sudden modification. What could be more matter-of-fact than a kick in the gut?

Max's rage lacerates the air. His tone, sputtering in ferocity, is fused with his helplessness. In the midst of the family he can swear with preposterous invective about them: "One cast-iron bunch of crap after another. One flow of stinking pus after another." The rhythms mount to tragic force; but the situation, and Max's inability to stand *alone* away from the family deny his stance. Pinter, however, never allows the rhetoric to become simply a burlesque. Max's words can sometimes strafe the truth, as when he confronts Ruth for the first time. The word becomes magical, not merely predictable bravado but something with the *potential* of illuminating the moment. When Max talks of life down at the paddock, the rhetoric becomes obviously sexual and necessary to buoy Max's limp libido. But there is more to it:

> MAX: . . . I always had the smell of a good horse. I could smell him. And not only the colts but the fillies. Because the fillies are more highly strung than the colts, they're more unreliable, did you know that? No, what do you know? Nothing. But I was always able to tell a good filly by one particular trick. I'd look her in the eye. You see? I'd stand in front of her and look her straight in the eye, it was a kind of hypnotism, and by the look deep in her eye I could tell whether she was a stayer or not. It was a gift. I had a gift.

The first "filly" we see Max judge is Ruth. He looks her straight in the eye and reports that she is a "smelly scrubber," "a stinking, pox-ridden slut." Typically, Max's rhetoric hides the need behind his response; but not so blatantly that we forget his words. Ruth may not be a whore, but she acquiesces to a *pied à terre* on Greek Street. Not only is Ruth highly strung, she turns out (temporarily at least) to be a "stayer." Here, for a moment, experience and the fantasy of rhetoric intersect, only to follow their particular vectors. But the fact that Max's

words somehow have a bearing on Ruth's final situation in the
house, that they echo through the play, reinforce the sense of
chance, the multiplicity of connotations, the importance of
environment to the *meaning* of a given word—all thematic
goals toward which Pinter has honed his vision:

LENNY: Make the beds.
MAX: Scrub the place out a bit.
TEDDY: Keep everyone company.

Max repeats words at the end of the play which have a totally
different meaning from the beginning. The "scrubber"—the
"slut"—is transformed into a new vernacular by the voracious
appetite of the family. Words, like the objects they define,
have a chameleon quality.

The rhythm which tempers the family's modest proposal is
half ironic, half truthful. And even in the last scene, Pinter
introduces a discord, a line whose tone and sincerity are indi-
cated by its tempo. Sam, who cannot stand this arrangement,
confesses *in one breath:* "MacGregor had Jessie in the back of
my cab as I drove them along." There is a pause. Then the
calculated, blunt beat of the family dialogue picks up as if the
impassioned words had not penetrated their linguistic game,
their scrupulous brutality:

MAX: What's he done? Dropped dead?
LENNY: Yes.
MAX: A corpse? A corpse on my floor? Get him out of
         here! Clear him out of here!

III

In a play so sensitive to words, it is not surprising that language is one of its major themes. Where most plays use speech
merely as the vehicle for ideas, Pinter sees it as a tuning fork
of the unconscious:

Life is much more mysterious than plays make it out to be.
And it is this mystery which fascinates me; what happens
between the words, what happens when no words are
spoken at all.*

The Homecoming exudes a passion for linguistic clarity and
shows the impossibility of precise definition. Ruth, for instance, concludes the new arrangement with the analytic, legal
patois whose passionless tone is in direct contrast to the play's
body of words:

> RUTH: All aspects of the agreement and conditions of
> employment would have to be clarified to our mutual
> satisfaction before we finalized the contract.

Max ends the play in a call for linguistic clarity. It is his passion and his fear:

> *Pause.*
>
> MAX: Lenny do you think she understands . . .
>
> *He begins to stammer.*
>
> What . . . what . . . what . . . we're getting at? What
> . . . we've got in mind? Do you think she's got it
> clear?
>
> *Pause.*
>
> I don't think she's got it clear.

It is pertinent that the philosopher, Teddy, the man who knows
how to use language, to operate on things as well as in them,
is the cuckold and ultimate fool. Teddy's words cannot explain
the family or its passions. Facts are never enough, but are the
only tool for explanation which is the household passion. Lenny

---

* John Russell Taylor, "Accident," *Sight and Sound* (Autumn, 1966),
p. 184.

asks his father for "the real facts about my background." Sam
reiterates his driving routes as if they were descriptions from a
Victorian novel. Max knows how to pick the horses as well as
Jessie's pale corded blue silk dress. He is the most practical and
the most ruthlessly specific:

> MAX: He didn't even fight in the war. This man didn't
> even fight in the bloody war!
> SAM: I did!
> MAX: Who did you kill?

Words become labels which simplify and control alien experience. Ruth, like any potentially dangerous object, is catego-
rized. Pinter dramatizes the process of *naming*. Lenny prefers
"Cynthia . . . or Gillian"—middle-class and slightly old fash-
ioned. Max, of course, wants the exotic "Spanish Jacky" to fire
his hothouse imagination. As with all the language in *The
Homecoming*, the terms suggested indicate the difference in
need.

Words, in Pinter plays, seem to have two distinct functions.
The first is as a gambit for emotional survival—the precision
which defeats. Ruth's tone with her husband contrasts glar-
ingly with the hard accuracy she uses with Lenny:

> LENNY: Good evening.
> RUTH: Morning, I think.

The second function of words is to reinvent the mercurial
world. Max's opening monologue to Lenny starts in the third
person, switches to a more intimate first person and then back
again. The variations in syntax indicate Max's isolation, his
movement from the real world of sad confrontation to an
imaginary one of painless victories:

> MAX: He talks to me about horses.

Pause.

I used to live on the course. One of the loves of my life. Epsom? I knew it like the back of my hand. I was one of the best-known faces down at the paddock. What a marvellous open-air life.

Pause.

He talks to me about horses. You only read their names in the papers. But I've stroked their manes. . . . I was the one they used to caH for. Max, they'd say, there's a horse here, he's highly strung, you're the only man on the course who can calm him.

Within the syntax, Pinter captures the hollowness of memory trying to forge itself into concrete forms. His language, like the objects he describes, is at once convincingly tactile and infused with potential for mystery and betrayal.

In the realistic environment of *The Homecoming*, Pinter revitalizes the currency of stage language, restoring it to spoken symbols where each word stirs up deep and far-reaching associations. The word, couched in silences from which it sluggishly emerges and buoyed by rhythms which make it rich in ambiguity, becomes an essential dramatic tool. By acknowledging its power (and limitation), Pinter's theater stoops neither to easy explanation nor decorative lyricism. The stage image is a careful amalgam of gesture and word. The counterpoint of physical movement and linguistic energy makes *The Homecoming* one of the most carefully chiseled plays of this century. By raising the poet's concerns of syntax and sound, rhythm and response to the level of public spectacle, Pinter has discovered his own territory—where there is a modern truth to be chronicled and where only his maturing linguistic sensibilities can journey.

AN ACTOR'S APPROACH

An Interview with John Normington

INTERVIEWER: Did your understanding of the play change between when you read the play and when you performed it?

JOHN NORMINGTON: The first time I read it, I didn't have any precise conception of what it was about. I was asked to read for the part and I thought it was for Lenny, or possibly Teddy. I didn't think it was for Sam.

INTERVIEWER: What did you think of Sam at first?

NORMINGTON: I had an idea of what Sam was about from the beginning. The final thing didn't turn out the same, as it was of a rather washed-out, a nasty, if anything, although pretending to be sweet, besieged old man who drove his taxis and was very proud of them. The nastiness of the character didn't hit me immediately. One of the first problems of playing the part was that, although in the early stages he might appear the victim, he was just as capable of putting the boot as the rest of them.

INTERVIEWER: Were things explained to you all, or were you left fairly much on your own?

NORMINGTON: It was like a voyage. Peter Hall didn't say, "This is what the play's about." And Pinter never does say what the play's about. We regarded the early rehearsals—and Peter was very good about this—as a period of exploration. We tried to see what the play would mean with the six people who were cast. What would come out of us.

INTERVIEWER: Did you have a variety of ideas?

NORMINGTON: Yes. Some obvious ideas. That it was a play

137

against women was suggested. That all the characters hate women, which is a glib one. We chucked that out fairly early. You tend to work just one side if you decide exactly what it's about.

INTERVIEWER: You wanted to keep it open to many possibilities?

NORMINGTON: We kept it open more or less all the time. We were lucky to have a reasonably long time—five weeks—in which to rehearse the play. And we were on the road for quite a bit.

INTERVIEWER: Did Hall talk to you about your performance? And Pinter? Did they give you notes about it to the extent that they wanted certain things to come out?

NORMINGTON: Yes. The obvious one was that I was playing a man of sixty-three. That was the least problem because I've played older parts before. The big problem was the tendency to make him the victim. I had played a lot of rather cuddly old men. I had trouble hitting this harsher quality. Not too harsh, because that wasn't the whole thing. But not to make him too round and too soft. I finally cracked it quite late in rehearsals. I suddenly hit on a walk for the old guy. I got this mental image of how he would sit when he was driving the taxi. He probably sat the same, more or less, all the time. At the edge of his seat, with one foot forward. That gave him a harder appearance. Harold concentrated on the text, the precision and rhythm.

INTERVIEWER: What were the rhythms that Pinter wanted to stress?

NORMINGTON: What Pinter wanted to stress—which doesn't strike you until the play is on—was a stylized naturalism. It was in fact natural speech rhythms. That is the way people talk.

INTERVIEWER: Extended over a long period of time?

NORMINGTON: Exactly. So you have to stylize. If you write down what people say at any precise minute, it will of course be boring.

INTERVIEWER: Did Pinter talk to you personally about your performance?

NORMINGTON: He was marvelously helpful. We were all very nervous of Harold. Peter was good because he kept calm. Harold and I made contact after a terrible rehearsal. It was quite dreadful; we had run through the play and it was not good at all. We went back to the dressing room. Vivien's very good on these occasions and she got the Scotch out and we all got a bit tight. Harold just said, "You can play this part. You will be marvelous in the part once you stop acting. Don't act an old man. You're doing it all now and we can see it all happening." This was obviously what I had been doing. Hitting on the walk late was fine because I had gotten over the idea of acting by then. What I was doing was coming on and saying, "Yes, I'm a young man really, but I'm being very old." The voice was old and the walk was a bit stooped and Harold just said, "You've just got to find yourself. You, John Normington, who isn't sixty-three but twenty-six. What you've got to say is, 'Here is Uncle Sam.' It's no use telling us how old he is until you've found him. To be in John Normington at twenty-six, he's got to be there." Looking back on what he said, it's not as clear as it was then. He came to the next run-through and it was the first praise I'd got, from Harold. It worked such marvels for me. Two or three of us hadn't got any praise up to that time. We hadn't been discouraged. Knowing Harold now, I don't think one would be so discouraged. He's not the sort of man who says "lovely, darling."

INTERVIEWER: Pinter's suggestions were very simple and direct?

NORMINGTON: Yes.

INTERVIEWER: You didn't ask for explanations?

NORMINGTON: Only once, and then I realized how pointless it would be. I asked if I died when I had my heart attack at the end. To which he said, "No, you're not living any more."

INTERVIEWER: In terms of the family you're not living any more?

NORMINGTON: Yes. He said, "You're not dead, but you're no longer living. You're just lying there." I must admit I didn't know what he meant. The whole part builds up to that moment. To do or say something positive. It's the only truthful thing he says in the whole play. But I don't think he's witnessed as much as he says. He likes to think he knows an awful lot. Whether he had witnessed the sexual act between Jessie and MacGregor in the back of the car, I don't know. But he does know that at some time, in the back of his car, they had it away.

INTERVIEWER: Is Sam just supposed to be a neuter or does Max's continual frustration about his own impotency influence the role he puts Sam into?

NORMINGTON: I discussed with Harold the accusations Paul makes about him—being a Sodomite, bending over—and I think he's not a Sodomite. If he's anything at all, he's neuter.

INTERVIEWER: Because the language invests him with a vitality he doesn't have?

NORMINGTON: Exactly. When he starts talking about Mac-Gregor, he picks up Max's rhetoric: "He was a lousy stinking rotten loudmouth." I would say that this is Sam's rather unsparkling and unwitty attempt at the game.

INTERVIEWER: Was this game something that you developed or that Peter Hall guided?

NORMINGTON: It was probably Harold and Peter who hit on this. It was thrown open one day at rehearsal. The big scene just before Ruth's entrance at the end of the play—the discussion of putting her on the game. It was being a terrible problem. Not just staging it, but how it should be played. Peter suggested that we try it as if no one meant anything they said, until Ruth's question: "How many rooms would this flat have?" The most shattering moment in the play.

INTERVIEWER: Because you know that she means it?

NORMINGTON: And that nobody else really does. It's really a game for Teddy, to see his reaction. It worked marvelously I thought, just watching it. It was terribly funny, but more horrific, because these people didn't mean what they say. That's when we hit on the idea of the game. That coffee scene, which was very formal, the exchanges between the two boys: ". . . take a table. Philosophically speaking. What is it?" "A table." This, we discovered, was part of the game. Lenny says, "Right, now here's what the game is. Put my brother on the spot. Let's make him look a cunt, because he is."

INTERVIEWER: Sam's relationship here is very interesting, because Sam also has an angle on Ruth. Ruth represents something to him. He, just as every other member of the family, wants something from her.

NORMINGTON: Yes, he wants someone to talk to. I'm sure it's nothing deeper than that. The way he hints: "I was taking care of her [Jessie] for you." I think all it means is that there was someone unaggressive, feminine.

INTERVIEWER: If we understand Jessie to be a pretty rotten dame, you were the fastidious housewife around the house?

NORMINGTON: I think I looked after her.

INTERVIEWER: She probably didn't clean up very much.

NORMINGTON: No, she left her cigarette ends on the floor.

INTERVIEWER: You were the one who picked up after her?

NORMINGTON: Probably, because—but one mustn't enter that homosexuality bit—the delayed homosexual return to the feminine figure is very important. You often find that homosexuals have deep relationships with women in a totally nonsexual way. This is probably Sam's thing.

INTERVIEWER: I presume that Sam is in the game all the time?

NORMINGTON: Yes, but he's very bad at it.

INTERVIEWER: Are you sure of that? He seems to be scoring lots of points off Max in his quiet way. He may be the weakest, but he alone is the possessor of the most powerful punch.

NORMINGTON: He can be good at it, especially with Max. But when you have a very big set game like the philosophy game or a very high-powered game like "what are we going to do with Ruth?" Sam says nothing at all. He can score off

Max all right, but only when he is talking about the one thing he knows about, which is Jessie.

INTERVIEWER: And ultimately he knows that Max is impotent.

NORMINGTON: They're both in the same boat!

INTERVIEWER: One of your last lines before you pass out is something I couldn't figure out. Sam takes Teddy aside and says: "You know, you were always my favourite, of the lads. Always. *Pause.* . . . You were always your mother's favourite. . . ." What is happening there?

NORMINGTON: At first I thought it was a funny attempt to make contact with Teddy.

INTERVIEWER: It's much stronger than that. Does it mean that Teddy is her only real son?

NORMINGTON: That was suggested. I think in a funny way, I'm attacking him for leaving the family. All the family feel rather badly that he's dared to break up the family unit and go away.

INTERVIEWER: Do you rule out the other interpretation entirely?

NORMINGTON: No.

INTERVIEWER: The whole question of the origin of families is the key to Pinter. It is interesting that the actors all seem very certain about the relationships, yet I don't think that Pinter believes in a historical or moral certainty.

NORMINGTON: No, Harold never intends to make anything as positive as that. Had we asked Harold, "Must I bring out that Jessie had one son with Mac, which is Teddy?" he would have said no.

INTERVIEWER: You say in the same speech: "When you wrote to me from America I was very touched, you know. I mean you'd written to your father a few times but you'd never written to me."

NORMINGTON: Yes, accusingly. I mean, "You bugger, you never wrote to me for a long time!"

INTERVIEWER: What about the Jewishness of the family?

NORMINGTON: Harold was very ambiguous about that. I think it's any family. But I think Harold's rhythms are English-Jewish. The actual rhetoric is very English-Jewish. A lot of English Jews are very enormous, orotund. Max doesn't just say, "I was a butcher, I worked very hard." He goes into this elaborate thing about the slab. English Jews often talk in a very detailed way. I'm from the North and it's very like the North. The English pattern of speech is to understate. The idiom is Jewish.

INTERVIEWER: That's enough to give the touch of a Jewish family to the play. Wouldn't an Englishman say there are Semitic roots here?

NORMINGTON: They would also say working-class roots. But also Jewish roots. I know Harold didn't want to stress that. We discussed whether we should use the Cockney Jewish accents. That was stamped on very quickly. Harold is Jewish Cockney. I think that is why his writing is so alive. It's very similar to working-class Northerners. They have this fullness of speech and this was bound to rub off on Harold.

INTERVIEWER: Sam's driving. He uses this driving in the family situation and it's his identity.

NORMINGTON: Yes. He thought he was better than anyone else because he was the breadwinner.

INTERVIEWER: For the others, you get the feeling that the game is a matter of life and death. Certainly Max would just disappear if he didn't have this masculine rhetoric to fool himself. Is your game as nasty? Or are you just playing it to pass the time or keep your head above water within the family?

NORMINGTON: It's survival from Sam's point of view. He's good at the game with Max simply because they're brothers and they've been at it ever since they could talk. He knows all his brother's weaknesses. That's why Sam doesn't contribute in a lot of the other scenes. He hardly knows any other members of the family.

INTERVIEWER: Does Lenny ever direct any remarks to Sam?

NORMINGTON: Yes, he's feeding for the game. Especially at

the beginning when he says, "Where have you been? . . . All the way up to London Airport?" He's making an opening for the game. Max immediately falls for it. He's seen the game start, he knows the cues.

INTERVIEWER: In the scene with the coffee and the cigars, you are sitting between Max on your left and Ruth on your right. Why was this arrangement made?

NORMINGTON: I think it was Peter's idea that it was Mum and Dad—Paul and I as a stage picture. The other boys are spread out. But in the center of the stage are the established figures, and the honored guest is in the best chair.

INTERVIEWER: It is so resonant and funny and phallic. At the end, when you pass out, what in the tension of the scene makes you fall and cop out of the game?

NORMINGTON: It's when Ruth says she will stay. I took that as my motivation, because I couldn't believe it. I didn't take the early part of the game very seriously, before Ruth comes down, about putting her on the game, and the flat. That didn't affect me. This was a rather nasty game that I was having no part of. But when she says she will, Sam decided this is the moment to bugger the whole thing up. I'll just tell her what happened to the other lady we used to have here.

INTERVIEWER: That's very antifeminist. You don't want another lady in the house if she is going to be a whore, which is what the other lady was.

NORMINGTON: He says it just to put a spanner in the works. Poor thing, it doesn't. All Max says is, "What's he done? Dropped dead?"

INTERVIEWER: How did you see their relationship there without a woman? How did you justify being all men alone for that time?

NORMINGTON: It seemed natural. On the surface they were very self-sufficient. Max could cook, I drive and clean up. Even Lenny says, "I'll have to Hoover that in the morning, you know." They are self-sufficient. I don't know whether Lenny used to bring women up secretly. Not for himself, but when he started to procure. Before he had flats.

INTERVIEWER: Max kids you about getting married: "When you find the right girl, Sam, let your family know, don't forget, we'll give you a number one send-off, I promise you." Is that rhetoric you've heard before?

NORMINGTON: Yes. I think it doesn't even hurt any more. Max is hinting at his effeminancy again. It's just another joke like, "You'd bend over for half a dollar on Blackfriars Bridge."

INTERVIEWER: But you really get back at him: "Nothing like your bride . . . going about these days. Like Jessie."

NORMINGTON: That's a nice comeback: look at you when you took a bride!

INTERVIEWER: Did performing in this play bring you to a more elaborate understanding of your craft?

NORMINGTON: Yes, after Harold's remark about acting an old man. Economy is the thing I've found. I realize now—if it's a marvelous play—what you need to do. Before I did *The Homecoming*, I thought it was necessary to Sell with a capital s. That you must really come on, make it absolutely clear what you are doing. This taught me how much the audience will come to you. They get far more involved if they're wondering why he's doing that or what he's going to be. It is much more rewarding, too. Finally it was a great help that the text was economical, but it didn't help me initially. The economy didn't hit me till quite late on.

INTERVIEWER: Is that because he didn't put any stops as to what you could do in the text?

NORMINGTON: Exactly. I felt I must invent something, thinking, now what can I do to convince the audience I'm sixty-three? It didn't hit me until the middle of the rehearsals that the text would help me to give a very understated performance.

INTERVIEWER: Could you give me a speech where your rhythms might have confused the issue.

NORMINGTON: The washing-up scene. Just before Ruth comes down, toward the end of Act One. They're very short exchanges, but I used to get them wrong. Sam's making as much noise as he can. He is banging about, just to get everybody upset. I am washing up, and I put the glasses down very definitely. Sam'd probably spend ten minutes wiping a glass so that everyone going in the kitchen would see that Sam was wiping a glass. That he's actually washed up. And I used to throw it away. I didn't get right in:

SAM: What?
MAX: What are you doing in there?
SAM: Washing up.

Paul and I had a lot of trouble with the rhythm of that.

INTERVIEWER: And the rhythm really is intended to show that you are doing a job which, as breadwinner, is not actually yours?

NORMINGTON: Exactly. And I used to tuck a towel into my trousers so that everyone would notice that I was doing something that should not be done by me.

INTERVIEWER: It is interesting that, as the passive member of the family, you are also the breadwinner. One would expect you to be in the kitchen.

NORMINGTON: Yes, because he's the most neuter, he would do the chores. But I think Sam very rarely cleans. He does, on certain mornings, wash up. We all get up terribly early. Teddy says to Ruth: "Have to be up before six, come down, say hullo." I think that on some mornings, Sam decides to get up before anybody else and wash up. And there'd be great banging and putting down of things.

INTERVIEWER: Did you come away with key ideas as to how to perform these kinds of plays?

NORMINGTON: Yes. It was without question the most enjoyable thing from an actor's point of view. We went through a lot of torture, because you always do. But I thought it was the most enjoyable because we felt like a string quartet. That we were very proficient. We could all play the score. We knew the tempos and we had our conductor. We all knew exactly what we were going to do. There was no "we'll try this tonight." We knew exactly, especially by the time we got to America, what we were doing at every single moment.

INTERVIEWER: You didn't really need an audience, like my father [Bert Lahr], who used to judge by audiences where he was going.

NORMINGTON: For reaction, we did need an audience, like a string quartet. If the audience is with you, then you will play it even better. But unlike comedy, where if you didn't get your laughs early on, it gets you down and you strain. We might have done this early on, on the road. There are some very difficult houses on the road in England. The first night in Brighton I shall never forget. There was no string quartet at all. The audience heckled and booed. While we were saying lines they actually shouted, "What nonsense! Oh, what rubbish!" They stormed out and there was no applause at all. Just an avalanche of boos. To which Michael Bryant, when we were taking the call, beamed and shouted quite loudly, "We're still being paid, thank you." Harold was delighted and I don't think he was pretending. Because it had precisely the effect on them that he wanted. Just absolutely hit them below the belt. I was frightened. We knew it was going to be tricky in Brighton. Peter came round and said, "I had a look at the house and don't expect a lot from them." They'd come in their tiaras and they only want Flora Robson.

INTERVIEWER: By the end do you think—and this is an individual question—that what began as a confused understanding of the play then developed into a complete understanding of what you had to demand—left you with any larger metaphorical meaning of the play? Do you see the play as anything more than people in a room in the natural dynamic of a family?

NORMINGTON: It certainly means more to me now than when we rehearsed it, when I first read it. Pinter is throwing things open. All I understand about the play is that it is an actor's dream. And I'm sure Lenny's speech about a night on the waterfront will be an actor's audition speech from now until the end of time. It's such a joy to play and I think it's very open. It's a very full play and you could read virtually anything about life into it.

INTERVIEWER: I don't think that Pinter is unconscious of these things, although he is dealing with concrete situations. By dealing with concrete situations, he doesn't leaden them down to eliminate all these other things. When I met him I said, "What do you make of all this business of being and not-being?" is a great put-on of existential philosophy. He said, "Well, I don't know, I've never read any." I can't believe that. I think he's very intellectual.

NORMINGTON: He is. He pretends he's a chap off the corner. He once said to a critic who asked him how close he was to Pirandello, "I've never heard of him." Of course he has.

INTERVIEWER: Doesn't Pinter almost help direct his plays?

NORMINGTON: He does, but he learned from directing *The Birthday Party* at the Aldwych that it doesn't quite work if there's just him directing it. That's why he asked Peter to direct *The Homecoming*.

INTERVIEWER: What do you think Hall added to the tone of the play? Do you think if anything was invented that Pinter didn't realize? Because I know that sometimes Pinter does not find things until after the play is on.

NORMINGTON: The whole style of playing the play—the string quartet—that's in Pinter, but Peter was the conductor. He invented the bar lines, gave it a frame, and paced it. The whole technical presentation of the play was Peter's.

INTERVIEWER: Did Peter Hall ever tell you what he wanted the play to look like? It seems he left it very open ended.

NORMINGTON: This is how Peter works. Funnily enough, he's a bit like Pinter; he's never definite. He'll never absolutely say to you, "This is what this means." He never gives you a through line in a pedantic way like many directors will do. He feeds you with tiny little ideas. Sometimes it comes off, sometimes it doesn't. He used the same technique on all of us. It was a marvelous working relationship between the six of us. We had a marvelous understanding with Peter and Harold of total open criticism. We all said exactly what we felt in the early rehearsals. Peter was more like a chairman than a director who says, "I see it this way." We all discussed and criticized our own work. Not the play. Toward the end of rehearsals, after you had said a speech, you knew whether it was right or not. Without question. It wasn't necessary for Peter to say "that was too slow," or "you didn't get the meaning of that at all."

INTERVIEWER: The explicitness of your understanding of the play was necessary to lead to the audience's understanding of the play's fundamental ambiguity. Whereas if you had played it ambiguously, it would not have worked.

NORMINGTON: We all started out on a real, immediate thing. On a clarity, which, I suppose, great ambiguities come out of.

INTERVIEWER: When Max says, "Then he'd dandle me. . . . Pass me around, pass me from hand to hand." That's not true?

NORMINGTON: No.

INTERVIEWER: But Paul would say, "But he hated his father and it's a real event." The difficulty in talking to actors is that in acting they see it as a real, truthful thing. But in fact, if you look at the language, it's very vague. It's not specific in the way that Pinter is specific—for instance in talking about Jessie's dress as being "heavily encrusted in pearls." But in playing it concretely there is an irony which comes out of the vagueness of the writing. He's believing in something that's just air.

NORMINGTON: From Max's point of view, he has to. If you start to say, "Well this is untrue, and from this moment on everything I say to that point is going to be untrue," I don't think it will come out as anything. The word ambiguous was never mentioned, but the greatest thing that comes out of the play is ambiguity.

INTERVIEWER: But as characters reacting to characters on stage, were you conscious of Lenny's make-believe? Or was it all very concrete to you?

NORMINGTON: It was all sort of probably real. No, when we were playing it, it was absolute fact. When Sam reacts to Lenny in the first act, we have a discussion about America, about London Airport. "I took a Yankee out there today."

INTERVIEWER: You went to London Airport and you stopped at the Caprice and he gave you a box of cigars. That's not make-believe?

NORMINGTON: No, he gave me the box of cigars. But whether we stopped at the Caprice and whether he said, "I was the best chauffeur he'd ever had"—well I mean, if you just pick someone up at the Savoy and take them to London Airport, it's unlikely he's going to say you're the best chauffeur in the world, isn't it?

INTERVIEWER: The actors respond as if there was no ambiguity. But Ruth sees through Lenny. She's always asking devastating questions.

NORMINGTON: Oh yes, she has a marvelous rapport right away. There's a wonderful moment when Ruth says, "How did you know she was diseased?" and Lenny replies, "I decided she was." Which is it exactly. That is the play, in the sense that it is true of every character that, whether it's true or not, you decide and make it true.

—INTERVIEWED BY JOHN LAHR

AN ACTOR'S APPROACH

An Interview with Paul Rogers

INTERVIEWER: Did Peter Hall begin rehearsals by explaining *The Homecoming*?

PAUL ROGERS: He did not give us a long lecture on it. This can be a help, but we knew the background against which *The Homecoming* was written. What Peter Hall did say, and this became abundantly clear, was that this is a play which is like a diamond, hard-forged after years of compression. Our job in rehearsal was to find as many facets as we could and decide which particular facet we would present. In the course of searching for this, I played Max many different ways, different emphases of character. What was presented to the public was surprisingly similar to my initial reading. My instinctive approach was very near to what Harold Pinter had in mind. Needless to say, the work in between made the final product richer. The line of the character was similar but the embroidery and the solidity of the figure was increased.

INTERVIEWER: You went to Pinter and asked him things. Did he give you answers?

ROGERS: Sometimes. Early in rehearsal, I misread Max's reverie about his father. I played that speech so that it became gradually more self-involved. When it came to the part where his father dandled Max on his knees, tossed him up in the air, etc., I had old Max in tears. It was such a moving thing. Pinter said, "No." And I said, "Jesus Christ!" I wanted the bloody actor to go. I finally took Harold by the coat lapels and said, "Tell me what it's about for Chrissake." He said one simple sentence: "He hated his father." And of course, obviously he did. It's a pitfall an actor can fall into, it shows that he hasn't completely absorbed the play as a whole. How could a family like this spring from anything but hate? It's a recurring theme. He loathes his father in the same way that the boys loathe Max. There isn't room for a moment of softness, for that kind of emotional reaction in any situation, even though it is pretended to.

INTERVIEWER: Then Max's speech is a put-on?

ROGERS: No. If you read it the way it comes out, you get a picture which we often forget. How terrifying grown-ups are in sheer size to a little child. You can imagine this great drunken bastard breathing Guinness fumes and Christ knows what and picking up this child. Poor little bugger didn't know if he'd come down in one piece. In point of fact, it's a memory of utter horror, fraught with fear, terror, and complete loathing.

INTERVIEWER: Are there things in *The Homecoming* which distinguish it as an actor's play?

ROGERS: A Pinter script contains all the bricks—all the straw and mud necessary to make the bricks. Every single part is a gorgeous one to play. There is no spare flesh, no wasted moment. The wonderful thing about Pinter is that he really writes about people. And the extraordinary way in which ordinary people's minds work. Ordinary people don't behave like people in a well-made play, where you follow one line of direction. Harold's plays are like a jewel box, they are so superbly put together. But the people in them are real people whose minds refuse to work along what are known as good, clear, dramatic channels. So the goodie is in the end pretty much recognizable as the goodie. A nonacting playwright can be a very responsible writer, but he doesn't have the feeling for the ultimate enjoyment of the performer. One is absolutely sure Pinter would be delighted to play any single character in his plays.

There was only one page of cuts from the original text. Where Sam talks about the trip to London Airport, describing the difficulties of the roundabouts and the other drivers was eliminated because it was irrelevant. Harold drove out to the airport while we were in rehearsal. He came back and said, "My Christ, it's all gone, they put up overpasses. No one would travel by that route." Everything in the play was tried and tested before we got it; everything was utterly speakable. There is not a single line which had to be cut in order to make it speakable. This is an actor's instinct. Ordinarily, you have to cut many things which will not fall off the tongue. In Pinter the words really do come off the tongue and teeth beautifully.

INTERVIEWER: Did you learn anything about acting from being in a play as difficult as this?

ROGERS: You learn something all the time until the end. Arrogance. Plain, bloody arrogance. I've played kings and tyrants, Lear, Macbeth, Hamlet, and God knows what. But never in a play was it essential in one's relationship to the audience to come and *be*, relentlessly, without a thought of playing for any kind of sympathy, to be utterly arrogant and sure of the play, of yourself and your own skill as a player. This is very valuable. It's the kind of thing that your intuitive star, the kind that just blazes there, has. They possess an arrogance, which is often very, very charming. It's so marvelous because nobody else has it. Ordinary people in the street don't have it. All of us had to have incredible arrogance. And we were thrilled to have it. We walked onto that stage, particularly in New York, and there was never, on that first night, a more arrogant bunch of players. It was essential for the quality of the play. I think that Harold is gloriously arrogant, and I use the word gloriously advisedly because he's got the quality of a newly honed razor. The difficulty with *The Homecoming*—all of us were afflicted with this— is the complete comma accuracy that is necessary for his plays. It's got to be comma perfect. There is no room for the smallest degree of license within a Pinter text.

INTERVIEWER: Does this give you a sense of freedom? Terence Rigby [Joey] claimed that it made him nervous and depressed because he had to fit so tightly into this clockwork.

ROGERS: I am capable of being very ill-tempered in rehearsals; I'm usually deeply ashamed when it happens. But in *The Homecoming* I had one moment where I was absolutely desolate—floods of tears and the bloody lot. I just could not learn the words to the bloody play, I couldn't get the damn things in the right order. I was upset because this damn play had infected us all in such a way that nothing less than perfect was going to do. There's an acting logic through the play—but oh my God, to find it! This was the shag—the plain mechanics of learning the lines.

INTERVIEWER: What does it mean in terms of performance if you have one idea of the play and Lenny has another?

ROGERS: I can't say what it would mean if you had a heterogeneous collection of actors. I was a new member of the Royal Shakespeare Company, but I'd been friends with Peter Hall for a long time and their style of working was nothing new to me because of my experiences at the Old Vic. This attitude is extremely workmanlike. You don't go in for any shim-sham schmaltz doubletalk before getting on with the job. It is positively dangerous to have an over-intellectualizing actor. They usually lose the bloody lot. I don't mean that stupid actors are good things, but if you're going to take your choice, choose a stupid one rather than an over-intellectual one, because it's quite possible that the stupid one will have a clarity of being which will allow various overtones and undertones and implications to come through unmuddied. The act of being an instrument—the clearer the tone, the better the thing—when playing. I think it's absolutely true of the whole team—certainly true of Vivien, who is the most masterly of Pinter players in that she never muddies her interpretation by any degree of intellectualizing at all.

INTERVIEWER: You also had to learn the pauses, too. That was part of the meaning wasn't it?

ROGERS: You can't continue a line until you've got all the substructure, the pauses, the rhythms. Otherwise the meanings of the words change.

INTERVIEWER: Is this an actor's impulse or a writer's instinct about life?

ROGERS: Very difficult to separate one from the other there. I'm sure his actor's instinct plays a large part in the making of his plays.

INTERVIEWER: The silence has become an idea in fiction and especially in Beckett. I think that Pinter understands this very well, because he's such a fan of Beckett's. He's really an intellectual but he denies it.

ROGERS: Merely because he has no use for the high fallutin' intellectual. He likes the practical intellectual. He doesn't care for intellectualization, which is where the intellectual goes off the rails so often. You can do it for fun from time to time, but it must always be known to be fun. He really puts old Teddy over the coals!

INTERVIEWER: Did you as an actor find difficulty with all the silences and pauses?

ROGERS: Yes. The challenges happen long before you present it to an audience.

INTERVIEWER: Does the fact that you have to live with these pauses make you react differently on stage? I get the feeling as a member of the audience that you're making up your mind as you go along at every point, that you could go one of four or five ways.

ROGERS: That's a good observation. Because, of course, that is what the characters are doing to each other.

INTERVIEWER: In other words, the silences are active things, they are part of the drama?

ROGERS: Absolutely. I said to Harold fairly early on, "One thing this play is not about is noncommunication. These characters know only too bloody well how to communicate." And Harold said yes. They communicate only too well because their very method of communication presumes a knowledge of the other. The silence or the pause is active and fulfills many purposes. From the simplest kind, where you leave a pool and say, "Fill it." "There it is, put something in it." "Let's see what we can make out of this one." Even the pauses are, in many places, malicious. Nobody else writes silences in that way. Pinter writes silences as a musician orchestrates pauses. The silences between bunches of notes are as important as the notes themselves. Most playwrights leave it to chance.

INTERVIEWER: Did Hall or Pinter guide you into the rhythm?

ROGERS: They chose the cast with great care to get the kind of actors who could work with them and were right for the roles. It's very common nowadays in the English theater for a director to apologize if he gives a line reading, even if it's by mistake. They want it to happen, but they don't want to impose it. Pinter will not interfere. You can ask him, but you will have to beg him for information. He's always fascinated by the possibilities of writer-actor-audience relationships. He's not going to allow anything to come between reactions within the triumvirate. A lot of people think that he's arrogant. There's a certain amount of truth to all that, thank goodness, because the really fine ones are pretty sure of their worth and it's proper they should be. But arrogance doesn't enter into his relationship with cast or director. He's much too excited about the process of discovery, what happens when a man walks into a room, or when he puts a snatch of dialogue on paper. Neither Hall nor Pinter gave indications of what they thought the rhythm of the line should be because they wanted us to find out from the text, within the context of the general shape of the play, of a particular sentence, how it went from A to B. They wanted us to find out—and this is really a kind of creative humility—it may be that your notion is only halfway there anyway. I'm sure he didn't know a great many of the implications in *The Homecoming* existed until after he had written it. Harold loves to watch and see what is going to happen. He is such a disciplinarian with himself that he will not allow himself to spoil the excitement, the pleasure of seeing what other dimension other people are going to give him. His fascination is such that he will let the other dimension become extraordinary, even touch madness in its intention, just to see where the process takes him. It often happens that he gets a dimension out of his work because a play is a combined effort and not the work of one man, as Gordon Craig would have had it. It's when you get a bunch of people you really respect, believe in, and trust—you then have an explosive mixture. You're right to rein yourself in as long as possible because the most extraordinary things can happen.

INTERVIEWER: Pinter keeps all dramatic possibilities open. As a consequence the play is concrete but has symbolic overtones. Yet as an actor you cannot play that. Once you start thinking about universal considerations, you start aiming for things.

ROGERS: Harold has the wit never to think about universal considerations himself—until long after he writes the play. The universal considerations are within him, as with any great artist. You have to do what Harold does, which is to leave air room, space for the metaphors.

INTERVIEWER: Did you make any addition to the character of Max?

ROGERS: Yes, the physical Max. I don't know whether it was in the printed edition, but it was very much in the directing —Max's clothes and appearance. He wears a cap which he never removes, a collarless shirt with a stud, a woolen long-sleeved cardigan, and he carries a heavy stick—more than a walking stick, but a walking stick. My additions came out of a knowledge of Max as rehearsals progressed. I thought his footwear should be eminently suitable to his function in the house, and very, very comfortable, for all his padding about in the kitchen, doing all the bits and pieces, and even going down the road to the pub. A pair of white canvas tennis shoes—a very old pair. And my other addition, which is not specifically stated, is that Max, being a butcher by trade, would be scrupulously clean in his personal habits. It's in the script that "He's obsessed with order and clarity." These clothes are very old. Cardigan darned out of its mind. But clean. His trousers were a great difficulty because the wardrobe mistresses would stick knife-edge pleats in and I'd say, "Jesus, it mustn't be that at all!" What Max actually did each night was put his trousers underneath the mattress, so there is this crease in them. They're not baggy, shapeless pants, they are neatly-creased trousers. These things mean more to the actor than to the audience. The audience observes the general picture. Max had clean nails, too, absolutely no sort of funereal nails. Hands scrupulously clean—again, the butcher. The butcher who is now working in the kitchen preparing the terrible dog's food. The trousers for me go back to the days when Max went up West with MacGregor and cut, I'm sure, no end of a figure. Those two characters, when they went up West, were just as spruce as Lenny is now.

INTERVIEWER: Did the other characters take as much care with their clothes?

ROGERS: If ever there was an indication that the two elder boys are mine and the younger one isn't, it's the fierce physical picture. Lenny is dressed in this beautiful silken mohair, in this incredible room. Silk shirt, silk tie. And Teddy is dressed with care, which is not necessarily part of your average American college professor. And there is a contrast with Joey, who is slovenly. I've never got Harold to say, but I don't believe Joey is Max's son.

INTERVIEWER: But Terence Rigby said, "It's all in the family."

ROGERS: We never forced that one on Terry. We didn't want to confuse him. We pulled his leg unmercifully, in fact treated him like Joey. Do you realize that Joey is the one person in that family whom they all really rather love?

INTERVIEWER: But you hit him pretty hard?

ROGERS: He exposes my fear of impotence. So I hit him where I know it will really get him, in the solar plexus. He goes down like a log. As a young man, I was all attack. I'm still all attack, but I'm seventy. Max resents the fact that he's seventy. What is fascinating is that he physically hits Joey, whereas

with the others, he attempts to destroy them in a really cruel
way.

INTERVIEWER: Is that because the only thing that makes an
impression on Joey is a physical blow?

ROGERS: No. Because you can make Joey look a most awful
fool. He does once or twice and Joey reacts—sort of. And then
there's a suggestion that there's real heart in Joey. This is expressed in his attitude to Ruth.

INTERVIEWER: He wants a mother?

ROGERS: Everything. I think Joey's in a way a very balanced
character. Almost sweet.

INTERVIEWER: In that respect he doesn't fit into this household?

ROGERS: I feel very strongly that Joey is MacGregor's and
Jessie's. I've always felt that there's this strange unity in the
family. They will destroy each other, but you let any outsider
. . . I think they'd just kill him. With Joey the family affection is so extreme, that it would be very violent. They don't
mind him being knocked about in the boxing ring, 'cause that
doesn't hurt, if you know what I mean. It's just funny that he's
a punchbag for all these characters. But Joey's more one of their
own than they are themselves. But he's really stupid—Mac-
Gregor a Scot and Jessie, and I think Jessie was a supremely
brainless woman.

INTERVIEWER: One gets the feeling that Max did all the work
or that Max was Sam, because Sam was a big confidante of
Jessie's.

ROGERS: I don't think that Sam was part of the household
when they were married.

INTERVIEWER: John Normington [Sam] thinks so because
he was such a confidante of Jessie's and that he did the actual
female household things because she was a slovenly dame.

ROGERS: I never knew that that was John's idea. My idea is
that Sam moved in when Jessie died because there was room.
I'd love to know what Harold feels. I think that the old bach-

elor was living in his own little room. But he was the sort who couldn't resist coming round and giving it all a bit of a stir every day. He was very much part and parcel of the whole thing although he didn't live there.

INTERVIEWER: You were very hurt by Jessie?

ROGERS: Not by Jessie, by MacGregor. And yet MacGregor was forgiven because MacGregor was his friend. It was almost the Eskimo attitude. MacGregor is still the friend, but behind there is the bitterness of betrayal.

INTERVIEWER: Do you think that the family is Jewish?

ROGERS: Harold has not made this evident, except in terms of the language. They don't take a Jewish standpoint, they don't mount any Jewish hobby horses. Like Harold's own family, they've lapsed. They're Jewish by descent, rather than by practice. If we believe that Jewry is a condition of religion and not race, then they're English. But to an English actor, it leaps out of the text—the facility of speech, the quality of speech and the area: North London, Hackney. Far more important than this family being Jewish is their instinct for family, family unity. In Anglo-Saxon terms, this isn't part of the blood and being. This to an English audience would telegraph a Jewish heritage. Our London Jews have more than a melodic line in the voice, there is a speech shape, it isn't a dialect, the speech is, as it were, foreign, in the way that English is foreign to a Welsh tongue. Not in terms of syntax or shape of the sentence, but merely in the sound. It's stylized and there's a suspicion of a lisp, which is very much to the point for a man of his age. But we avoided all those things. The Jewishness came out of the rhythm of the speeches and the way that the speeches were put together. The repetitions, the emphases upon certain aspects. The ironies, that curious, very unEnglish working of the mind.

INTERVIEWER: Even the aggressiveness isn't English. That butting in and fighting.

ROGERS: In that way, it most certainly isn't. Although certain breeds of Englishmen are very aggressive. But it's the humor, the flair for the word.

INTERVIEWER: When you struck out at Joey that was the first time that you'd done anything large. All the gestures that you expect to be large—a leg, a glass—were movements but on the smallest scale. Within the framework of the play they have a certain gigantic quality, which is an actor's achievement. My father used to say that a good actor could hold the audience's attention by just standing on stage.

ROGERS: Quite right. Harold said the most exciting thing: a man comes into a room—marvelous! What's going to happen? Drama immediately. The door is open, the person is in, the door is shut. Huge question.

INTERVIEWER: For instance the first words when you come into the room: "What have you done with the scissors?" Right away, great drama. Is this your way of bugging Lenny?

ROGERS: I'm slaving my guts out. Making this delicious meal which very shortly he is going to say is dog food. What does he think he's doing sitting on that sofa reading the *Racing Times*? In this family everyone needs to be acknowledged within his own function.

INTERVIEWER: Pinter is saying you want attention. Here you are, head of the family and he's not paying any attention to you.

ROGERS: But that is unthought by the character. It is the motivating thing *underneath*. What you see is literally what happens. A disgruntled old man comes in who wants to cut something out of the newspaper and at the same time to be a bloody nuisance. This is nothing Pinter's dreamed up. The nicest of parents do it.

INTERVIEWER: You said that it was Ruth's homecoming, not Teddy's. Did Pinter point this out to you?

ROGERS: He didn't point it out, but he applauded it when we found it. It's Ruth's homecoming right from the moment when she comes in through that door. It appears to be Teddy's homecoming, but he's long turned his back on that.

INTERVIEWER: But he has come out of his way to come back?

ROGERS: Yes, and I think this is very typical of the family—just the malicious delight of going back, knowing what's going to be there, and presented with a fascinating problem—Ruth—to see what happens. He suspects that the result on Max will be very much worthwhile. Teddy has not got the intelligence of Max, but he has got the family fiber which enables him to stand up to everything they throw at him.

INTERVIEWER: In a way he's insulated by his position, which is above them. His knowledge gives him a certain kind of arrogance—which is why he's virtually cuckolded in a classical tradition. He's intellectually arrogant, but he lacks a certain kind of innate life.

ROGERS: That's half the story, the other half is that his marriage was finished long before they left the States. So what he appeared to be losing, what the family appeared to be taking from him, was in fact gone already. From their first entrance they're obviously not talking to each other. When I say "not talking" I'm using it in the broadest sense—they have no communication.

INTERVIEWER: In what way is it apparent from the beginning that it is Ruth's homecoming?

ROGERS: Typical Pinter. Marvelous little hints. The strongest one is that she goes out for a walk. It's two o'clock in the morning and in that area of London you can easily get lost. It's a labyrinth. She says later on that she grew up close by. There's another in that scene between her and Lenny, when he does all of the talking and whenever she does speak she cuts everything straight through. That indicates that not only is she very much in control of the situation as woman versus man, but this kind of approach doesn't upset her. She knows the argot; all the stuff he comes out with to try and shock her isn't going to shock her at all because her background has hardened her against that kind of shock. Like the story of the lady underneath the arch —that kind of thing cuts no ice with her.

INTERVIEWER: Each of you has a different relationship to Ruth, yours is a romantic kind of hothouse thing, and Joey says "Gillian."

ROGERS: Which is the sort of name you associate with a nice

English girl. A touch above Joey in class. But Max is certainly the reverse of a romantic attitude—Spanish Jackie is most crude.

INTERVIEWER: When you challenge Ruth, is this your way of introducing her to the game? We know from her first shot with Lenny that she's very able to take care of herself.

ROGERS: No, this is my opening attack on Teddy. She's a means to an end. I don't know where she comes from, I don't know what kind of girl she is. Max is only interested in how Teddy will respond. It's my big attack on him for treating me and the family in the way that he has.

INTERVIEWER: At the end of the first act you begin to square off. Now this is a kind of ritual battle isn't it?

ROGERS: Oh, but it isn't a question of fighting.

INTERVIEWER: But at least in the American production, he rolls up his sleeves and then you move around. That's not in the stage directions?

ROGERS: No. You remember that the invitation was to give his old father a kiss and a cuddle. And at the end of the act, they're absolutely four square with each other and Teddy says, "Come on, Dad. I'm ready for the cuddle." And it means cuddle. It doesn't mean I'll knock your block off. It means I *could* knock your block off, you silly old bastard. There is an ambiguity there, as with every word they utter. Max brings the curtain down with a roar of delight and triumph: "He still loves his father!" And he does. When I first read the play, I said, "Harold, I think this is a play about love." He said, "Right." Now we're talking about a very curious kind of love. Not even a betrayal of love. It's the basic thing that holds a family together. In some cases it's need, convenience, and so on, but particularly with this mob there's a tremendous hard core of a thing which can only be described by the word love. One of the most evocative things about this family is, ". . . we all sit round the backyard having a quiet gander at the night sky."

INTERVIEWER: Do you think they actually do this?

ROGERS: Yes. This is a very strange family. One important

aspect which Harold kept hammering was that this is a very lovely family, his words were "It's a fine old mob." And he was not being completely facetious. Indeed, they sit in the backyard on a fine summer's evening.

INTERVIEWER: But you can't believe that any of them appreciated nature. They were all too busy fighting. As a performer you can believe in the family, but the audience, by the very nature and environment of the play, puts all that into question. As with the speech about the baby being dandled, you can say that's very nice, but there's more than a touch of irony.

ROGERS: You couldn't really think it was very nice because it was spoken with utter and complete loathing. This is not the entire life of Max's household. I think it is very wrong to think that it is impossible for that family which you see, under certain stresses, to be quite peaceful. But when they were sitting in the backyard, I shouldn't think six words passed between them. They weren't consciously communing with nature, it was just nice and comfortable and because they're a family, and it had always been done, they put the chairs in a circle. And what I said about love and hatred being so near that you could put a hair down the middle, this is it.

INTERVIEWER: Do you feel that with Max's relationship to his sons—there is in the rhetoric of violence and hate a certain kind of affection?

ROGERS: I would be chary of using the word "affection." I would use the word "love." They are interdependent, not for the ordinary things of life, just for the game they play, which is their life. They can't survive without it. Teddy's whole reason for coming back is to participate. The outcome of that confrontation between Max and Teddy is an absolute understanding between the two that indeed Teddy went off, became a professor, a scholar that they were proud of, but didn't come back, so they weren't proud of. In fact, they despise him. He's the one with the brains, so they despise and admire him. Married without telling me, occupied a most interesting position without giving me any information, three grandchildren whom

I was not informed about. When faced with that sort of thing, he is the Old Ted, he really is the son, and in that curious way he does love his father.

INTERVIEWER: In America, this idea of "game" is associated with improvisation.

ROGERS: This game is the opposite of improvisation, in their original basic rules. The rules of this game are that nobody ever shows a blow actually register. Improvisation comes after that, with the acceptance of the rules. But these unspoken rules hold out and are the bones on which the game is played. But you improvise even with games that have strict rules, like soccer, Rugger, American football, etc. The skill lies in the improvisation.

INTERVIEWER: What constituted an improvisation within the rules?

ROGERS: Sam's marvelous talk about what a lovely woman Jessie was. The turn is on what a swine Mac was.

The cheese-roll is a bit of a break in the rules, and Lenny's reaction. But it's strictly within the rules that Lenny chooses to make a full scale drama out of a bloody roll and a piece of cheese—that this man's wife and the cheese-roll are equated at the same moral level.

The setting up of Ruth is a really outrageous piece of improvisation where Lenny and I vie with each other to see how far we can go A) to astonish each other, and B) to see whether we can get Teddy. Whether we can get both of them, because by then we've realized she's fighting, too. What more outrageous suggestion can you make to a man, particularly if he's a member of your own family, than that proposition? That since she's so free and easy with Joey, why not really make a going concern of this thing? Where they're really hoisted by their own petard is when she comes down. She's come home. She knows this area, these people, this behavior—this attitude, to a lesser and greater degree of cruelty, is something which is very much of the Cockney mind. It isn't a strange dramatic form that Pinter elected to use, it is firmly based in reality. In terms of a

Jewish family, it is caused to a certain extent by the ghetto situation. Cruelty is very much part of the humor in that part of London. This kind of ribbing. Pinter and his group really go at each other in an unbelievable way. So this, to a London audience, needs no explanation. They're not Cockney, they're Cockney once removed. A Cockney is anyone born within the sound of Bow Bells, and depending on which way the wind is blowing, Bow Bells can be heard a hell of a long way.

The game, the energy which goes into the destruction is sexual completely. It takes the place of any real confrontation, it is a form of sublimation.

INTERVIEWER: It is interesting that everyone else is impotent except for maybe Joey, who's a kind of brute sex, but perhaps he's the product of brute sex—MacGregor and Jessie. But everyone else is impotent.

ROGERS: Sort of, in one way or another. Max is, Sam is neutral.

INTERVIEWER: John Normington feels that because Sam sort of fills a function in the house—he's the one legitimate breadwinner (Lenny's a pimp)—he becomes a curious combination of father in the household and mother to the extent that he is the one who goes in to wash the dishes. Does that seem sensible to you at all?

ROGERS: That is a marvelous point of view for John to have taken as an actor. It's very much the point of view that Sam has got. But it has no actuality at all whatever. But it's a wonderful indication that John got right inside the character. Sam's contribution to the household in terms of moneymaking from outside is negligible. He just about pays his own way. I was a butcher, and in England we have never heard of a poor butcher. Butchering in this country is one of the richest trades. And Harold agrees with this, because there is another point where he is very keen to be understood. The condition of the room we live in is like that because we like it like that. It isn't a slum. It isn't filthy. I would love to walk into Lenny's bedroom because I think Lenny has wall-to-wall carpeting and the most marvelous furniture. To walk into Lenny's place would be like walking into another world. I think it's almost decorated. And Max has a wardrobe upstairs, I'm sure, of clothes that he can still get into and which are splendid and very expensive.

INTÉRVIEWER: This is still a lower-class family though?

ROGERS: It isn't even lower-class. This is a difficult one, in as much as it is Jewish, it doesn't fit into the English pattern of society.

The accents they employ because they wish to, because any-body in this country can speak as they will, it's very simple to change one's accent. The one I speak with now is as natural as the one I was born with, West Country, which is very near to American, which is why I can play American parts. They wear the kind of clothes that they wish to wear, not forced to wear by circumstances of poverty. I think stashed under the floorboards in my bedroom is an enormous amount of money. He sold that business and with all the goodwill and with what he had put aside, Old Max is very well off. But you aren't told that.

INTERVIEWER: And you don't necessarily believe it, because maybe this deal with the continental butchers is a lot of hooey.

ROGERS: Anyway, it didn't take place. But it didn't destroy his butchery job. I don't think the whole thing was necessarily make-believe. There was a certain framework of truth.

INTERVIEWER: I thought that Lenny was the bastard, be-cause he continually raises the question of being his father's son. "That night with Mum, what was it like?" Why does he ques-tion his origin? He may be his father's son, but he suspects that he isn't?

ROGERS: I don't think he suspects he isn't for a second. He knows perfectly well, they're too similar.

INTERVIEWER: Except that your reaction to him is amazing. He says to Max, "Look, why don't you just . . . pop off, eh?" Max says, "Pop off?" and Lenny goes into this thing about his background and then at the end: ". . . I thought I'd pop it to you." "Pop" being sexual—at least in American slang.

ROGERS: No, you "pop the question" in England.

INTERVIEWER: It's also father.

ROGERS: I don't think that either of those are relevant here. Much more to the point in terms of English is that it's such a trivial word. Silly little word to use when you are facing somebody with an absolutely devastating question.

INTERVIEWER: Why would he ask it at that moment?

ROGERS: You have to go back to the scene before. He's just been torn to pieces by Ruth with a glass of water. She has exposed utterly the fact that he is a pimp and impotent. He's absolutely stark naked and scared. When I come down the stairs, it's a turning of his own impotence by insulting. He's insulting me as a father. I'm impotent too at seventy, and therefore past it, and so he selects the most vividly wounding thing to liberate himself from what has gone before. I can't tell you how difficult it was, in the early stages, to justify just standing there. And there was one point—actually in performance, not just in rehearsals—when I literally used to boil and boil until the spit in the face. But that was absolutely dead against Max's character. I think it's honors between Lenny and myself. I have one terrible edge on Lenny. Lenny is more or less sexually incapable—often one of the by-products of being a pimp. He's a voyeur, a setter-up. Max can come back at Lenny; surely this is shown throughout the script. The only person he is incapable of coming back at is Ruth. And on this occasion—when Lenny asks him that devastating question—it's a matter of standing there. It's not a matter of defeat at all. The statement "You'll drown in your own blood" is, if you read it in those terms, a pretty fair commentary. Your own loathing will be your destruction. This is no capitulation. And the spit expresses that that is all he is prepared for. That is the only reading, otherwise there is no strength in either. The whole power of this play is that nobody must be defeated until the end. That was a mistake I was dangerously near making.

INTERVIEWER: Although Sam can protect himself with the one fact he has, yet he is vaguely defeated?

ROGERS: There are two absolutely stark bastards in the play. The biggest bastard of all is Teddy, the other is Sam. Sam is a swine; when he appears to be defeated, he isn't; he's like a midget sitting on an atom bomb.

INTERVIEWER: Pinter said to me that if ever there was a villain in the play, Teddy was it.

ROGERS: He is the biggest bastard of the lot. Of the fire-proofed collection, he is the most. He must never be played that he is. It must never be played with a leer to the audience, or you'll ruin it all.

INTERVIEWER: MacGregor is also a fantastic force—almost the ruling idea in that household.

ROGERS: When Peter Hall was given the play to read by Harold, he met him, bubbling with excitement and said, "What do you think of MacGregor?" He really wanted to know what Peter's feeling was about MacGregor. He's the leading character.

Sam knows that I know about MacGregor and Jessie. But when he says "Like other people," I play the game straight back into his court: "Other people?" And he doesn't dare to take the game any further. What Max is inviting him to do is to tread the tightrope further. In the end he does the inexcusable and passes out. Because he's broken the cardinal rule of the game, he just faints. He's broken the rules and he's not dead, he'll get up in a minute. And in medical terms the best thing to do for a faint is to leave him alone. But it's important to know that most of these things are not new; these attacks are old games.

INTERVIEWER: But Lenny and Ruth have a different thing going?

ROGERS: Except that the game Lenny plays with Ruth is the oldest in the world. But something new has entered the home which has been kept out. The house has been sterile from any woman's influence.

INTERVIEWER: Was that conscious, because of his betrayal earlier?

ROGERS: Yes, they made it so that no woman would live there. They knocked down that wall to make one big room. It looks like a waiting room. That's the way they like it, clear and masculine, like a butcher's shop. No nonsense and in a condition which would be repellent to the female mind. A nice touch in John Bury's set was the girder which nobody ever bothered to plaster over. It's doing its job of holding the house up and that's that. And under that terrible gray paint, they'd only bothered to put one coat on, they'd slapped on some whitewash, and underneath is a flowered wallpaper with large yellow roses. They'd thrown out all her rubbishy bits of furniture and kept all the things that were comfortable. His chair. It's my house and we'll get rid of that other rubbish.

INTERVIEWER: Terence Rigby [Joey] threw me off terribly because he believed everything at face value in the play.

ROGERS: Very right that he should. On one level he's right. One level of this play is uncomplicated—accepting the kind of family that they are, and by God, they exist. Accept that and there is one level in this play which is very straightforward. It is all explainable, understandable. This is the level that Terry was living on and it's the level that all of us had to start from and were lucky if we could get to.

INTERVIEWER: When you come down Lenny says, "That night with Mum, what was it like? Eh? When I was just a glint in your eye." That seems to imply that you're not his Dad?

ROGERS: There is no question that Lenny is my son, and it's because of that that he throws the question in my face. Lenny and I are so alike it's terrifying. But Joey. Teddy is very much one of us, very much Max's son. His other environments have provided him with a different set of weapons, what gives it the edge is the old family home. Teddy is an absolute match for the lot of us. If anybody really wins, it's Teddy, by the whole seduction. He's not unscarred, but that scar'll be mended by the time he's halfway across the Atlantic.

INTERVIEWER: When the curtain comes down at the end of the second act, everyone is frozen so beautifully, as in a fresco,

by that chair. And yet you know that everyone will reg... .
but you have been deposed.

ROGERS: I wonder frankly whether Max has got very much
longer. I think that Lenny's remark "You'll go before me,
Dad" is only too damned true. If he does, she's going to take
over. Forever or for three days? That's the point; it could be
either. That girl is perfectly capable, after three days of quietly
and completely dominating that household, of packing her case
and following Teddy. On the other hand, she could stay put.
Remember she has come home.

INTERVIEWER: Ruth, if she is just a regular housewife, knows
an awful lot about whorehouses and about being a woman of
the street. Because when she demands a room, she wants a
room that is a courtesan's special.

ROGERS: Aren't you over-simplifying the mentality of the
modern housewife? She knows about the whole set-up, how
whores live. This is the sort of girl that sixty to eighty percent
of your daily housewives know about from reading the papers.
There's Harold's great remark about Ruth lying on the couch
and Joey rolling on top of her: "There's only one thing extraordinary about that behavior, and that is that the rest of the
family happen to be standing around. That is the only thing
that is remarkable." He's absolutely right. There are people
rolling with gentlemen on couches by the dozen at that moment in New York and very few of them were their husbands.
And when you're talking with Ruth, remember her background.
It's a darn sight rougher than you think it is when you first meet
her. Her background was very poor and she came from the East
End of London. She's a girl who's learned to speak well.

INTERVIEWER: You have this wonderful speech where you
say: ". . . don't talk to me about the pangs of childbirth—
I suffered the pain, I've still got the pangs. . . ." You are both
mother and father. You're talking to Ruth and you're topping
her because you have her function.

ROGERS: It's a great scene because he's trying to find the
chinks.

INTERVIEWER: In the end, when you are on your knees to her, the game has broken down?

ROGERS: Oh, yes, in the sense that she's accepted and I didn't expect her to accept, and he's gone and I didn't expect him to go. As far as I, Max, am concerned, the end of the play is far more shattering than it is to any audience. It is completely and utterly and catastrophically unexpected. But the game is still proceeding when Max is talking about the photograph, which he knows is outrageous. You don't just say, "Would they like to see a photo, do you think, of their grandfather?" The game is played straight back at him by Teddy as cool as a cucumber saying, "They'll be thrilled."

INTERVIEWER: That gives Teddy somewhat of a victory?

ROGERS: By leaving, yes. As far as I am concerned, there is a question as to whose victory it is. Ruth and Teddy have a victory. Sam has a victory to the extent that he is not claimed by the new situation. He has copped out, or at least, he's neutral.

INTERVIEWER: So the question is whether it's going to be your defeat. Will she kiss you? That is the first time you are really "down."

ROGERS: Harold doesn't know what happens after that; neither do I. That's where Harold chooses to leave us. Max is in a moment of absolute defeat. Yet it was Harold's wish that you should feel the aggression, so that the words are a demand, not a request.

INTERVIEWER: Although it's a command, there is also a fear. Because he's on his knees and she's looking away stroking another man's hair.

ROGERS: In England, in the first production, I collapsed in the middle of that first tirade, or at the end of that tirade against her, when I say, "she'll do the dirty on us." I fell on my knees—in other words, it's a bit of a stroke—and I crawled right past Sam and said the speech from that position. Now this was Harold's intention, and while it worked in England, for the States we questioned whether we weren't over-emphasizing, as it didn't really achieve sympathy. The audience wasn't in any mood to be sympathetic toward Max and perhaps it would conjure up an unnecessary and irrelevant revulsion that, unless it was played with extreme care, might bring a laughter that Harold, at that moment, didn't want. That's why we limited the collapse so that it's not a collapse of supplication, but he just can't stand up, he's weak suddenly. This is important because although I was never allowed to overplay, it was unmistakably a stroke. And then we said, no, that's too hard and fast, there must be an element of doubt. And there's something that you haven't seen before in the play, and that's fear. Max is afraid and it's expressed in the words "I'm not an old man," which actually is a very simple expression of an emotion that is so complex that you couldn't express it, and at the same time there's this absurd awareness that physically he's going.

INTERVIEWER: And so the kiss becomes many things—a new unit, a new solidity of the family, an acknowledgment of his own sexuality, an attempt to make him whole.

ROGERS: All those things and on top of that, the simple one of "You bitch, you will not win. You bitch, I will be what I am in this household." Max was going to carry on until his dying day.

—INTERVIEWED BY JOHN LAHR

PINTER THE SPACEMAN

John Lahr

The human condition, Heidegger says, is to be there. Probably it is the theater, more than any other mode of representing reality, which reproduces this situation most naturally. The dramatic character is on stage, that is his primary quality: he is there. . . .

—Alain Robbe-Grillet, *For a New Novel*

While the new novel has set out to paint the surfaces of the object world, doing for literature what primary structure has done for sculpture, the drama of Harold Pinter has come closest to capturing the changed relationship between man and nature as the basis of the artistic experiments in the other arts. Pinter is a storyteller, not a scientist; but his images chronicle a world beyond the Newtonian perspective.

In the Renaissance, Shakespeare could make Hamlet tell the players the function of their drama—confident in man's direct relation to Nature and dominance over it:

. . . the purpose of playing, whose end, both at the first and now, was and is, to hold, as 'twere, the mirror up to nature; to show virtue her own feature, scorn her own image, and the very age and body of the time, his form and pressure. . . . (III, ii, 20–23)

Language, like the stage, informs the audience of man's sovereignty over the natural world, where he is both distinctive within it, and yet apart from it. Newtonian physics changed that view, its implications reaching far into the art of the twentieth century and the responses of its audience:

> [It] saw in man a puny irrelevant spectator (so far as being wholly imprisoned in a dark room can be called such) of the vast mathematical system whose regular motions according to mechanical principles constituted the world of nature. . . . The world that people had thought themselves living in—a world rich in color and sound, redolent with fragrance, filled with gladness, love and beauty, speaking everywhere a purposive harmony and creative ideals—was crowded into minute corners in the brains of scattered organic beings. The really important world outside was a world hard, cold, colorless, silent and dead. . . .*

Armed with a faith in reason and the mathematical certainty of the universe, the arts imposed on their varied images boundaries of implied coherence. History could be recalled and clarified, the future carefully charted. If the novelist could scavenge his memory or society for "truth," the picture frame gave the painting a spatial order where the objects fitted smoothly into the environment of the canvas, limiting the spectator's vision and controlling it. The proscenium stage imposed a certain formula on performance as well as on the play. The well-made play, with its careful architecture, its "plot points," its clear motivation, was the embodiment of a scrupulous logic which affirmed a middle-class in the passive stability of the world.

Harold Pinter denies the human animal its deterministic response; his characters are no longer stimulated to act out of a clearly defined past, but rather out of the vagaries of the moment. They defy theatrical convention—passing out on stage without being carted off, refusing to explain themselves, telling stories which merge ambiguously into fantasy. In denying ex-

---

* E. A. Burt, *The Metaphysical Foundations of Modern Science*, Doubleday Anchor Books, Garden City, N.Y., 1955, pp. 238–39.

plicit knowledge, Pinter finds laughter and dramatic content by inverting literary and stage clichés. His characters, caught in the web of their own rational powers, continually latch onto a certainty only to destroy it, root up objects only to find them change before their eyes. Although critics score Pinter for being "slow" or "unexciting," in fact, Pinter has released the world and its objects into a nervous uncertainty on stage which offers more variety and surprise. Far from being "absurd," his plays mirror a world which modern science has confirmed. "Observation means interference with what we are observing. . . . Observation disturbs reality." * Although the statement refers to the scrutiny of atomic particles, science has put into serious question the concept of an objective distance. "The act of observation is at the same time unavoidably an act of participation." ** As a result, the uncertainty of objects is not merely a fashionable esthetic, but a scientific fact. As Werner Heisenberg, the formulator of the Uncertainty Principle, has pointed out:

> . . . We are involved in the argument between nature and man in which science plays only a part, so that the common division of the world into subject and object, inner world and outer world, body and soul, is no longer adequate and leads us into difficulties. Thus even in science the object of research is no longer nature itself, but man's investigation of nature. Here, again, man confronts himself alone.†

Nature exists in Pinter's plays with no anthropomorphic overtones. It holds none of the lush benevolence of a Shakespearean bower nor does it offer the tenacious personal challenge of a Hemingway safari. Nature is primarily a memory in a claustrophobic urban world. The "pathetic fallacy" is not only forgotten, it is parodied. Goldberg, in *The Birthday Party*,

---

* Floyd W. Matson, *The Broken Image*, Doubleday Anchor Books, Garden City, N.Y., 1966, p. 127.
** *Ibid.*
† Werner Heisenberg, quoted in Floyd W. Matson, *op. cit.*, pp. 128–29.

recalls that pastoral moment: ". . . I can see it like yesterday. The sun falling behind the dog stadium. Ah!" When Lenny recalls the out-of-doors in *The Homecoming*, the purifying salvation of nature is mocked by his specific fantasy of violence:

> LENNY: I mean, I am very sensitive to atmosphere. . . . For instance, last Christmas I decided to do a bit of snow-clearing for the Borough Council. . . . What I anticipated with a good deal of pleasure was the brisk cold bite in the air in the early morning. . . . Bloody freezing. Well, the lorry came, I jumped on the tailboard, headlights on, dipped, and off we went. Got there, shovels up, fags on, and off we went, deep into the December snow, hours before cockcrow. . . . an old lady approached me and asked me if I would give her a hand with her iron mangle. . . . I said to her, now look here, why don't you stuff this iron mangle up your arse? Anyway, I said, they're out of date, you want to get a spin drier. I had a good mind to give her a workover there and then, but as I was feeling jubilant with the snow-clearing I just gave her a short-arm jab to the belly and jumped on a bus outside. . . .

The rooms which enclose Pinter's dramas are pierced with no sounds from an outside world. There is no "breaking string" to warn of impending chaos, no twitter of birds as a harbinger of a new day. In Pinter's newest play, *Landscape*, the title implies that Pinter has finally taken his characters out-of-doors. He hasn't; instead, he shows us the mind recreating the outside world, painting it vivid and soiled. Duff and Beth speak, but do not listen to one another. Beth recreates the golden stillness of a beach; Duff relates how he went to the duck pond to feed the birds:

> DUFF: Mind you, there was a lot of shit all over the place, all along the paths, by the pond. Dogshit, duck-

> shit . . . all kinds of shit . . . all over the paths. The
> rain didn't clean it up. It made it even more treach-
> erous. *Pause.* The ducks were well away, right over on
> their island. But I wouldn't have fed them, anyway. I
> could have fed the sparrows.*

The coarseness is hilarious, carefully counterpointed with
Beth, who in her dreamy delicacy doesn't hear it. The precision
of Pinter's language paints Nature with graphic clarity; but they
are in a room, talking. Both worlds become real; both characters
are charged with a relationship the audience can never verify.
Does the landscape exist as they see it? Is it totally apocryphal?
What is most important is only that they see it. Pinter's advantage over the new novelists is the stage itself; he can show the
breach between man and the objects of his environment,
dramatize a very special understanding of the process of perception. Robbe-Grillet, with many of the same modern instincts
—conscious of geometry (specific groupings in Pinter) and the
object world—describes life outside the mind not merely with
microscopic particularity, but enmeshed in a cerebral vision.
The difficulty of conjuring a sense of three-dimensional space
on the page is immense, if not impossible. In Robbe-Grillet's
Jealousy, for example, jungle noises are outlined with a precision which always seems to have designs upon the reader:

> Still, all these cries are alike; not that their common
> characteristic is easy to decide, but rather their common
> lack of characteristics: they do not seem to be cries of
> fright, or pain, or intimidation, or even love. They sound
> like mechanical cries, uttered without perceptible motive,
> expressing nothing, indicating only the existence, the posi-
> tion, the respective movements of each animal, whose tra-
> jectory through the night they punctuate. . . .**

---

* Harold Pinter, *Landscape and Silence,* Methuen, London, 1969.
** Alain Robbe-Grillet, *Jealousy,* in *Two Novels by Robbe-Grillet:
"Jealousy" and "In the Labyrinth."* Grove Press, New York, 1965, pp. 49–50.

The contemplation does not startle; nature is not *shown*,
only described. The intention is diminished by the form. This
is perhaps why Robbe-Grillet turned so effectively to film and
why Marguerite Duras has experimented with the stage. Objects in space are dramatic; man's reaction to them is theater.

In Pinter's plays, the perceiver is the active agent; his values
and his actions are not comprehensible by some external be-
havioral pattern, an objective rational force. Pinter dramatizes
what physiobiology has demonstrated, "that there can be no
genuine understanding of behavior without an understanding
of the *behaver—on his own terms*." * In Pinter, the audience
only knows what it sees happening on stage; no sociological
assumptions are allowed. *The Homecoming* seems elusive where
it is merely being realistic; it refuses to offer up experience to
the audience from a point of view. Instead, action is fractured
by the complex private manner in which each character reacts
to what happens on stage. The play is beyond moral questions
which demand precisely this single perspective. In *The Homecoming*, Ruth leaves her husband and children to live in Max's
household. Pinter does not intend her to be a whore (although
most American audiences reacted this way). She responds to
life on private, ultimately inexplicable terms. Her life in
America is arid, her husband egotistical and unthinking; but
her words offer only hints of the bleakness which no one else
(not even Teddy) can understand:

> RUTH: I was born quite near here.
> *Pause.*
> Then . . . six years ago, I went to America.
> *Pause.*
> It's all rock. And sand. It stretches . . . so far . . .
> everywhere you look. And there's lots of insects
> there.

---

* W. H. Ittelson and Hadley Cantril, *Perception*, Doubleday & Co.,
Garden City, N.Y., 1954, p. 7.

Pause.
And there's lots of insects there.
Silence.

In the same way, Max stalks his domain, swinging his cane
with the lingering memory of sexual potency. Hating women
and fearing them, he lives in a perpetual state of siege and yet
longs for contact:

MAX: I'm not an old man.
       He looks up at her.
       Do you hear me?
       He raises his face to her.
       Kiss me.

Max's suspicions, the fear and violence which dominate his
reactions, are never certain to the audience, only to him. They
see only a man clinging tenaciously to a sense of his own virility (". . . I always had the smell of a good horse. I could
smell him. And not only the colts, but the fillies . . ."), whose
reactions go beyond sentiment, interpreting every action with a
specific aggression. Sam, Max's brother and a chauffeur, insinuates that Max's wife and his best friend are having an affair.
Late in the play, as Sam passes out on stage, he confesses that
the friend made love to Max's wife, Jessie, in the back seat of
his car while he drove. True or false? We don't know. What is
important is that it seems true to Max, whose fear of it makes
it real. Early in the play, Sam jabs him pointedly with a pause
in which he chooses his words carefully:

MAX: Above having a good bang on the back seat, are
       you?
SAM: Yes, I leave that to others.
MAX: You leave it to others? What others? You paralysed
       prat!
SAM: I don't mess up my car! Or my . . . my boss's car!
       Like other people.

MAX: Other people? What other people?
       Pause.
       What other people?
       Pause.
SAM: Other people.

The word "boss" is sounded out slowly by Sam; it is too close to "brother" not to upset Max and unleash his questions.

If Pinter's drama seems to diminish the possibilities of experience—a criticism often leveled against it—in fact, he opens up a new, more illuminating mode of stage action. Where Beckett's philosophy must finally reduce itself to voiceless inaction (he has written a thirty-second play), Pinter opens up the stage to the examination of a new dimension of man's free will —smaller, perhaps, than the grand designs of earlier centuries, but one where variety, choice, and personal value still have an interest and a validity. This parallels new scientific defections from Gestalt theory of perception, in which there is a mutual determination of form (organism) and environment:

> What is significant . . . is the thesis that the individual is in the fullest sense an *actor* (not a mere field or receptacle), who creatively determines his environment by selecting and reconstructing the materials of experience in terms of his own sensitivities and makeup—his unique personal perspective. "What the individual is," in G. H. Mead's words, "determines what the character of his environment will be. . . ." Man sets the universe out there as like himself in matter and substance.*

Pinter is fascinated by the highly discriminating way in which man chooses to see the world. Man reconstructs the world and its objects through carefully selected stimuli. Ruth, calling attention to her legs, illustrates the point precisely:

---

* Floyd W. Matson, *loc. cit.*

RUTH: Look at me. I . . . move my leg. That's all it is.
But I wear . . . underwear . . . which moves with me
. . . it . . . captures your attention. Perhaps you misinterpret. The action is simple. It's a leg . . . moving.
My lips move. Why don't you restrict . . . your
observations to that? Perhaps the fact that they move
is more significant . . . than the words which come
through them. You must bear that . . . possibility . . .
in mind.

Ruth's sexy legs make the audience and the characters sali-
vate with lust. She makes her point. In the same way, Teddy is
held up for ridicule because, as a philosopher, he will not
acknowledge the autonomy between the objects which sur-
round man, and man himself. Objects in the world are both
nonreferable and mercurial ideas which he refuses to compre-
hend:

TEDDY: There's no point in my sending you my works.
You'd be lost. It's nothing to do with the question of
intelligence. It's a way of being able to look at the
world. It's a question of how far you can operate
on things and not in things. I mean it's a question of
your capacity to ally the two, to relate the two, to
balance the two. To see, to be able to *see!* I'm the
one who can see. That's why I can write my critical
works. Might do you good . . . have a look at them
. . . see how certain people can view . . . things . . .
how certain people can maintain . . . intellectual
equilibrium. Intellectual equilibrium. You're just
objects. You just . . . move about. I can observe it.
I can see what you do. . . .

Pinter's irony is twofold: not only is Teddy cuckolded, but
the stage is inundated with situations which deny his way of
seeing. A glass of water turns into a sexual threat ("Lie on the
floor. Go on. I'll pour it down your throat"); a cheese-roll is

equated on a moral scale with a man's wife; a large ash tray held by Ruth receives the ashes from each of the men's cigars with a sexual longing that vanishes as quickly as their configuration in front of it.

The sense of chance, the arbitrariness of nature is shocking and visually breathtaking in Pinter's plays. He is able to create an expectation of some large physical gesture as the logical extension of the emotional tension on stage (a brawl over the wife, for instance). He then turns table on the audience by having his characters focus on something *small* (the cheese-roll). This is not a technique special to Pinter, but he does it differently. In *Hamlet*, for instance, the Prince, realizing the sword has been poisoned, says, "The point envenom'd too! —Then venom, do thy work!" (V, ii). The sword is vitalized by Hamlet's purpose; Hamlet sees the poison and the sword as extensions of *his* revenge. The audience expects him to run the King through. He doesn't; he grazes the skin. The revenge has an intellectual satisfaction for Hamlet in keeping with his cerebral temperament. The death will be slow—and savored. The King, by his own words, is merely "hurt"; Hamlet forces him to drink the poisoned wine which has killed his mother. The audience expects a large gesture—to see the King skewered and writhing in violent action. Instead, the gestures are small, almost intimate. The effect is overwhelming. The contrast yields its special insight.

Unlike Renaissance thought, Pinter will not allow his characters to see anything as the extension of their "purpose." The objects are silent; they offer no hint or omens, no final sense of connection in the chain of things. In *Landscape*, Beth makes a comment which elaborates Pinter's deep-seated distrust of an objective relationship to the world, and the insinuating appeal of such assumptions:

BETH: I remember always, in drawing, the basic principles of shadow and light. Objects intercepting the light cast shadows. Shadow is deprivation of light. The shape of the shadow is determined by that of the object. But not always. Not always directly. Sometimes it is only indirectly affected by it. Sometimes the cause of the shadow cannot be found. But I always bore in mind the basic principles of drawing. *Pause.*

So that I never lost track. Or heart.

The "principles" of drama, like the principles of Newtonian physics, offer an image of purpose, a clarity and simplicity which has insulated man from his world. In streamlining his plays, pruning the clutter of objects as well as words, Pinter focuses on the dynamics of perception, isolating special objects more easily for public scrutiny. "The only play which gets remotely near to a structural entity which satisfies me is *The Homecoming. The Birthday Party* and *The Caretaker* have too much writing. I want to iron it down, eliminate things. . . ." *
The silences and pauses have become bolder and more evocative in the process. This structured counterpoint to Pinter's words and gestures etch his unique world. The silences are different from those of Beckett, not simply a cosmic void or the final humming breakdown of "communication." Pinter's characters communicate clearly; people hear each other, only to misinterpret the words for their own emotional reasons. More important, the silences emphasize the element of perception. The characters are making decisions, weighing the balance, as the action is in the process of unfolding. These are *active* silences underscoring the intense inner life of Pinter's drama.

The artifice of immediacy is as important to Pinter's vision as it is to the new novelists. Pinter's characters are continually reconstructing the past from memory, unable to verify it or be certain of any origins except the present. Pinter's tactile, sensuous language insinuates a sense of reality into their vague imaginings. Max remembers his father with vivid words which have the sound of clarity, but whose logic denies it:

---

* Harold Pinter, quoted in Laurence Bensky, "The Art of the Theater 3," *Paris Review*, No. 10, Fall 1966.

MAX: Our father? I remember him. Don't worry. You kid yourself. He used to come over to me and look down at me. My old man did. He'd bend right over me, then he'd pick me up. I was only that big. Then he'd dandle me. Give me the bottle. Wipe me clean. Give me a smile. Pat me on the bum. Pass me around, pass me from hand to hand. Toss me up in the air. Catch me coming down. I remember my father.

The graphic language flushes the past into the present—or tries to. Pinter is able to create that rare sleight of hand which conjures a sense of the past without having to bow to history's chronology. Bombarded by stimuli, faced with a stalemate between man and the world, the present moment is the only dramatic situation which is justified by the philosophic implications of Pinter's vision. Similarly, Robbe-Grillet, in discussing his film *Last Year at Marienbad*, maintained significantly that:

> The Universe in which the entire film occurs is, characteristically, in a perpetual present which makes all recourse to memory impossible. This is a world without a past, a world which is self-sufficient at every moment and which obliterates itself as it proceeds.*

The same seems true of Pinter, except that on the stage even this intended immediacy comes closer to an audience's responses. If memory is impossible, man's reliance on it and its misuse are an interesting focus of drama which Pinter will not, wisely, disregard. In Pinter's closed rooms, the threat is not simply physical violence but the thought of change which takes place every second on stage. Pinter's drama attests to Natalie Sarraute's esthetic, which seeks "some precise dramatic action shown in slow motion," where "time was no longer the time of real life but of a hugely amplified present."**

---

* Alain Robbe-Grillet, quoted in Gore Vidal, "French Letters," *Encounter* (December 1967), p. 19.
** Natalie Sarraute, quoted in Gore Vidal, *ibid.*

Pinter inverts the techniques of inner monologue. The characters' soliloquies are never clear mirrors to their real feelings. Instead, the monologues teeter between private consciousness and public threat. In *The Homecoming*, Max comes downstairs, disturbed by the sounds coming from the parlor. He talks to his son Lenny in the third person, a manner of address which makes an audience wonder if Max is talking to himself or threatening Lenny:

> MAX: He wakes me up in the middle of the night, I think we got burglars here, I think he's got a knife stuck in him, I come down here, he tells me to pop off.
> LENNY *sits down.*
> He was talking to someone. Who could he have been talking to? They're all asleep. He was having a conversation with someone. He won't tell me who it was. He pretends he was thinking aloud. What are you doing, hiding someone here?

Neither the past nor the present is explained through Max's ruminations. The audience, however, is lured into the limbo of the ambiguous tone: an eternal present. The effect is different from the Elizabethan soliloquy, for instance, which usually brought the actor downstage away from the action. It was the external expression of an internal thought. When Hamlet speaks to the Ghost in front of his mother, the audience *sees* that he is talking to somebody; and that he is far from mad. His mother cannot see the Ghost. It is Hamlet's greatness and dignity that he can see further and more perceptively than those around him. The audience accepts this dichotomy; they are given a special access to "truth," hearing everything, seeing all the possibilities. The mirror is held up to nature for *their* benefit; the tragic "catharsis" also affirms a unity.

In Pinter, the audience experiences only what the characters do. They are privy to no extra information, no other choices. Pinter constructs a situation where fantasy has the weight of fact, and fact has the metaphoric potential of fantasy. There is no longer the Newtonian Chinese puzzle about appearance and reality. The "subjective" world and the "real" are not simply confused, they are combined. The character has no significance beyond what is presented on stage; he simply *exists*. Lenny's muscle-flexing tales of violence for Ruth, Max's monologue on Jessie's clothes (he calls her a "slutbitch" seconds later) show the capriciousness of imagination while focusing the audience's attention on these changes of perception from moment to moment. The only facts we can know are that the characters change their minds, that they say one thing and do another, that their dreams are not synonymous with their actions. Pinter refuses to comment on them, to favor one over another, because to do that would be to point to a moral or opt for a certainty which his plays deny.

It is interesting that *Landscape* extends the technique of dramatic inner monologue further than he has taken it before. In this short play, Pinter indicates no concrete theatrical gesture, only characters facing each other obliquely, speaking in realistic argot which turns in on itself and destroys the boundaries of the concrete. The mystery and the "reality" of the characters develop as they explain themselves, each speaking in his special tempo. Pinter indicates his intention in the stage directions:

> DUFF *refers normally to* BETH, *but does not appear to hear her voice.* BETH *never looks at* DUFF, *and does not appear to hear his voice. Both characters are relaxed, in no sense rigid.*

Pinter wants to retain the naturalism in order to work against it, blurring reality's framework. How much of Beth's romantic reverie is make-believe? How many of Duff's bravura tales of pub life are true? Everything remains uncertain—experience riddled with sexual longing, loneliness, hope, violence, but never offering itself up neatly for easy consumption. The drama is in the language:

DUFF: This beer is piss, he said. Undrinkable. There's
nothing wrong with the beer, I said. Yes there is, he
said, I just told you what was wrong with it. It's the
best beer in the area, I said. No it isn't, this chap
said, it's piss. The landlord picked up the mug and
had a sip. Good beer, he said. Someone's made a
mistake, this fellow said, someone's used this pintpot
instead of a boghole.

Experience and individuals are tumbled together; Duff's
voice absorbs the world. The audience must struggle to keep
identities clear.

Just as the stylized speech in *The Homecoming* kept the
audience poised on the immediate moment of dramatic reference, waiting for the carefully spoken words, forgetting about
the past to make sense of the present, *Landscape* shows Pinter
toying with the relationship of the audience to the stage illusion. Unlike the impressionistic naturalism of Chekhov, Pinter
deprives the audience of its traditional perspective—its distance—which can bring all the small strokes of the piece
together in a coherent pattern. Pinter forces the audience
toward the center of his drama, denying their position outside
the conflict. Crammed close to the stage image, the audience
can be inundated with stimuli without having the final say on
the final experience, without being able to make "sense" of it,
merely responding to the exigencies of action. With the present
and the past, the imaginary and the real so carefully wedded,
Pinter forges a unity which is undeniable. These are the "facts";
these are the ambiguities. That is all there is, and all we, as the
audience, should demand to know. Like primary sculpture, the
experience exists only within its own context, on its own terms.
In refusing to discuss *The Homecoming*, Pinter has said, "I've
nothing to say about *The Homecoming*. It exists and that's
that." * His words are specific and in keeping with his vision.
He talks about his play as an object in space in the same way

---

* Harold Pinter in a letter to the author (February 12, 1968).

as a sculptor or painter might. Pinter, who sees himself as a conventional playwright, has not completely disregarded the accoutrements of the past, but uses them against themselves, employing illusion in order to destroy it. This idea is prevalent among the innovators in the visual arts who have, however, denied the past and illusion. As Frank Stella has maintained:

> I always get into arguments with people who want to retain the old values in painting—the humanistic values that they always find on the canvas. If you pin them down, they always end up asserting that there is something there besides the paint on canvas. My painting is based on the fact that only what can be seen there *is* there. It really is an object. Any painting is an object and anyone who gets involved enough in this finally has to face up to the objectness of whatever it is that he's doing. If the painting were lean enough, accurate enough or right enough, you would be able to look at it. All I want anyone to get out of my paintings, and all I ever get out of them, is the fact that you can see the whole idea without any confusion. . . . What you see is what you see.*

In the same way, Don Judd's primary structures are based on an instinct which Pinter would concede—the autonomy of the object world. As a dramatist and an actor, Pinter responds to the stage environment and is conscious of his audience. In this sense his art differs from Judd's highly cerebral but path-finding extension of sculptural possibilities. But the reaction to Newtonian physics is an articulate part of both arts:

> JUDD: The qualities of European art so far. They're innumerable and complex, but the main way of saying it is that they're linked up with a philosophy—rationalism, rationalistic philosophy.
> INTERVIEWER: Descartes?
> JUDD: Yes.

---

* Bruce Glaser, "Questions to Stella and Judd," *Art News*, September 1966.

INTERVIEWER: And you mean to say that your work is apart from rationalism?

JUDD: Yes. All that art is based on systems built before-hand, *a priori* systems; they express a certain type of think-ing and logic which is pretty much discredited now as a way of finding out what the world's like.

INTERVIEWER: Discredited by whom? By empiricists?

JUDD: Scientists, both philosophers and scientists.*

Judd's objects are self-enclosed and nonillusory. Although people may walk around them, the object never is intended to say anything, except to indicate what it is. Like Robbe-Grillet, this becomes the sculpture of surfaces and geometrical rela-tionships—a precise, irreducible object. Judd indicates his con-cept this way:

A shape, a volume, a color, a surface is something itself. It shouldn't be concealed as part of a fairly different whole. The shapes and materials shouldn't be altered by their context. One or four boxes in a row, any single thing or such a series, is local order, just an arrangement, barely order at all. The series is mine, someone's, and clearly not some larger order. It has nothing to do with either order or disorder in general. Both are matters of fact. The series of four or six doesn't change the galvanized iron or steel or whatever the boxes are made of.**

The public often balks at art's attempt to show man the autonomy of things. When *The Homecoming* opened on Broadway, *The New York Times* printed a fatuous piece on what seven of the city's chic people thought was its "meaning." Many of them listed their findings in numerical order—precisely the way of thinking which Pinter's play strains to break. In the same way, critics of Judd's sculpture will not let it *be*; in observ-

---

* *Ibid.*, pp. 56–57.
** Bruce Glaser, *Don Judd*, Whitney Museum of American Art, New York, n.d., p. 10.

ing it, they exhibit the fatal tendencies which the art stands against:

> If they [the gallery-goers] care to disobey the rules, more-over, and meditate on the symbolism of Judd's boxes, the possibilities are endless. What is a box, they say, if not a coffin, a house, a treasure chest? As for that series of boxes climbing up the wall, what is it but a machine-produced, twentieth-century revision of a medieval illu-minator's stairway to paradise?*

In moving away from an anthropomorphic art, Judd and Pinter share similar instincts of the culture. Often attacked as "boring," "monotonous," "cool," "inhuman," they are the most human of artists, forcing open consciousness into new ways of seeing. Both artists shy away from universal "truths" in their respective work. "I couldn't begin to think about the order of the universe, or the nature of American society. I didn't want work that was general or universal in the usual sense. I didn't want to claim too much." ** Judd's words illustrate the predica-ment of conscience at the basis of Pinter's theater. There is not much one can claim for the world, but only a smaller, private detent between its objects and oneself. As in Pinter's play, where no proscenium arch is able to limit the variables of action, the three-dimensional sculpture has an infinite variety of angles and perspectives. It cannot be identified; it does not affirm any order but its own interrelation of parts, color, scale, material. Where the earlier plays of Pinter evoked the environment and its insubstantiality, *Landscape* obscures even that aspect of existence. The stage direction reads: "The background of sink, stove, etc., and a window is dim." Beth and Duff are not conscious of the boundaries of their room, but exist outside them. Part of the chimera of environment is not merely that it may change before one's eyes, but that it may bear no relation to man at all. This development seems to parallel Judd's interest in objects defin-

---

* *Time*, March 22, 1968.
** Glaser, *Don Judd, op. cit.*

ing a three-dimensional space. "Obviously, anything in three dimensions can be any shape, regular or irregular, and can have any relation to the wall, floor, ceiling, room, rooms or exterior or *none at all.* . . ." *

The stage allows Pinter to give this vision, shared by such a variety of artists in different fields, a scope and dimension the other experiments cannot claim: he can translate the *process* of nature's ambiguity with a directness and immediacy that the others have, as yet, not been able to accomplish. It is his art which approaches the dynamic of scientific insight which so many of the genres invoke. He has not merely broken with the past, but used the conventions of an old world-view to illustrate their limitations. While man exists on this planet, language and gesture, objects and esthetics will abound. Pinter, by showing the failure and strengths of the human equipment, hints more precisely at what is "out there." His plays demand of life no new meanings, simply new questions.

---

* Glaser, *Don Judd, op. cit.*, p. 12.

BIBLIOGRAPHY

WORKS BY HAROLD PINTER
PLAYS
The Birthday Party. London: Methuen, 1965.
The Caretaker. London: Methuen, 1967.
Landscape & Silence. London: Methuen, 1969.
The Room & The Dumb Waiter. London: Methuen, 1966.
The Tea Party and Other Plays. London: Methuen, 1967.
The Collection & The Lover. London: Methuen, 1964.
The Homecoming. London: Methuen, 1964.
A Night Out. London: Samuel French, 1961.
Old Times. London: Methuen, 1971.
Slight Ache and Other Plays. London: Methuen, 1961.

POETRY
Poems. Edited by Alan Clodd. London: Enitharmon Press, 1968.

MEMOIR
Mac. London: Emmanuel Wax for Pendragon Press, 1968.

CRITICISM
FULL-LENGTH GENERAL STUDIES
ESSLIN, MARTIN. *The Peopled Wound*. London: Methuen 1970.
   Pinter: A Study of his Plays. London: Eyre Methuen, 1973.
HAYMAN, RONALD. *Harold Pinter*. London: Heinemann Educational, 1968.
HINCHCLIFF, ARNOLD P. *Harold Pinter*. New York: Twayne Publishers, 1967.

INTERPRETATIONS

ESSLIN, MARTIN. "Harold Pinter." in *The Theatre of the Absurd*, pp. 205–223. Eyre and Spottiswoode, London, 1962.

LAHR, JOHN. "Pinter's Room: Who's There?" *Arts Magazine* (March 1967), pp. 21–23.

———— "Harold Pinter." In *On Contemporary Literature*, pp. 682–689. New York: Avon Books, 1969.

MAST, GERALD. "Pinter's Homecoming." *Drama Survey* (1968), pp. 266–278.

MORRIS, KELLY. "The Homecoming." *Tulane Drama Review* (Winter 1966), pp. 185–91.

PESTA, JOHN. "Pinter's Usurpers." *Drama Survey* (Spring 1967), pp. 54–65.

SCHECHNER, RICHARD. "Puzzling Pinter." *Tulane Drama Review* (Winter 1966), pp. 176–84.

STORCH, R. F. "Harold Pinter's Happy Families." *The Massachussetts Review* (Autumn 1967), pp. 703–12.

REVIEWS

New Statesman, 69 : 928. June 11, 1965.

New Republic, 152 : 29–30. June 26, 1965.

New Yorker, 4 : 50, July 31, 1965.

Time, 89 : 43. January 13, 1967.

Newsweek, 69 : 93. January 16, 1967.

Saturday Review, 50 : 51. January 21, 1967.

Hudson Review, 20 : 105–107. Spring 1967.

Commentary, 43 : 73–4. June 1967.

PINTER ON PINTER

"The Art of the Theatre 111," *The Paris Review*, No. 39, pp. 13–37. Interview of Harold Pinter by Lawrence M. Bensky.

"Writing for Myself," *Twentieth Century*, CLXIX, 1008, (London: February, 1961), pp. 172–75.

"Writing for the Theatre," *Evergreen Review*, No. 33, (August-September 1964), pp. 80–82.

"Pinter Between the Lines," *The Sunday Times* (March 4, 1962).

Manuscript notes and a page of typescript from *The Homecoming* reproduced in *The London Magazine* New Series, No. 100, July/August 1969.

Biographical Information

PETER HALL. Formerly the managing director of the Royal Shakespeare Company. Was made a CBE, 1963. Mr. Hall has directed Shakespeare's History Cycle at Stratford-on-Avon and *Hamlet* with David Warner. At the Aldwych Theatre, he directed Henry Livings' *Eh?*, Gogol's *The Government Inspector,* and Pinter's *Landscape* and *Silence.* At the Royal Opera House, Covent Garden, he directed Schoenberg's *Moses and Aaron* and Mozart's *The Magic Flute.* He was given the London Theatre Critics' award as Best Director for his productions of *The Homecoming* and *Hamlet.*

JOHN BURY. Began his stage career as an actor with Joan Littlewood's Theatre Workshop in Stratford East. He designed for them over fifty productions including the original presentations of Shelagh Delaney's *A Taste of Honey* and Brendan Behan's *The Quare Fellow* and *Oh What a Lovely War.* In 1964, he was appointed Head of Design for the Royal Shakespeare Theatre. His designs for them included Peter Hall's Shakespeare History Cycle, *Hamlet,* and Pinter's *Landscape* and *Silence.*

PAUL ROGERS. Came to the Royal Shakespeare Company to play Max in *The Homecoming.* An alumnus of the Bristol Old Vic, he has played Shylock, Henry VIII, Falstaff, Macbeth, Iago, Cassius, Bottom, and King Lear. His films include: *Our Man in Havana, Billy Budd, The Trials of Oscar Wilde,* and *The Looking-Glass War.*

JOHN NORMINGTON. Joined the Royal Shakespeare Company in the 1963–64 season. With them, he has played Antipholus of

Epheseus in *Comedy of Errors;* Glendower in *Henry IV, Part I;* and Justice Shallow in *Henry IV, Part II.* His films include: *Inadmissible Evidence* and *The Reckoning.*

Contributors

STEVEN M. L. ARONSON. Is an editor and critic.

MARGARET CROYDEN. Is Assistant Professor of English at Jersey City State College and is a frequent contributor to leading newspapers and magazines. Her articles on theater have appeared in the Sunday *New York Times, The Village Voice, Saturday Review, The Nation, The Antioch Review, The Texas Quarterly,* and the *Translantic Review.* Her book on the avant-garde theater is soon to be published by McGraw-Hill.

BERNARD F. DUKORE. Is the recipient of a Guggenheim Fellowship (1969–70) to write a study of George Bernard Shaw's dramaturgy. He has written *Bernard Shaw, Director* and edited (with John Gassner) *A Treasury of the Theater,* Volume II. He is executive officer of the Ph.D. program in theater at the City University of New York.

MARTIN ESSLIN. Critic and head of sound drama for the B.B.C. since 1963, is the author of the influential *The Theater of the Absurd,* and *Bretch: A Choice of Evils.* He is a regular contributor to a number of periodicals including *Encounter, Plays and Players,* and *The New York Times.* Mr. Esslin's most recent book, a study of Harold Pinter's plays, *The Peopled Wound,* was published by Methuen.

ROLFE FJELDE. As part of an extensive series of new Ibsen translations, Mr. Fjelde has published *Peer Gynt* in verse as well as two volumes of the major prose plays, and has edited the Twentieth Century Views critical essays on Ibsen. His poetry and criticism has appeared in numerous literary reviews; his plays have been performed at the Eugene O'Neill Foundation. He is a Professor of English and Drama at Pratt Institute in New York City.

JOHN LAHR. Is contributing editor to *Evergreen Review* and writes a weekly drama column for *The Village Voice*. He is the recipient of the 1968-9 George Jean Nathan Award for Dramatic Criticism. His books include: *Notes on a Cowardly Lion, Up Against the Fourth Wall, Showcase* 1: *Plays from the Eugene O'Neill Foundation* (editor). Mr. Lahr is Literary Adviser to Lincoln Center and General Theater Editor of Grove Press. He has written an award-winning film with John Hancock: *Sticky My Fingers, Fleet My Feet.*

JOHN RUSSELL TAYLOR. Is film critic of *The Times*. His books include: *Cinema Eye, Cinema Ear; The Rise and Fall of the Well-Made Play;* and *The Angry Theatre.* He has contributed to *Encore, The Times Literary Supplement, London Magazine,* and *Sight and Sound.*

AUGUSTA WALKER. Is a novelist. Her books include *Around A Rusty God, The Eating Valley, A Midwest Story,* and *A Back-Fence Story.* She has contributed stories and articles to numerous quarterlies.

IRVING WARDLE. Is the drama critic for *The Times* and editor of *Gambit.* He is currently writing a biography of the avant-garde producer George Devine.